TIMELESS PATTERNS
IN TIME

CHASSIDIC INSIGHTS INTO
THE CYCLE OF THE JEWISH YEAR

Volume 1

Adapted from the Published Talks
of the Lubavitcher Rebbe
Rabbi Menachem M. Schneerson שליט״א

PUBLISHED AND COPYRIGHTED BY:
KEHOT PUBLICATION SOCIETY
770 EASTERN PARKWAY
BROOKLYN, NEW YORK 11213

5753 • 1993

TIMELESS PATTERNS IN TIME
Volume 1

Published and Copyrighted © by
"KEHOT" PUBLICATION SOCIETY
770 Eastern Parkway • Brooklyn, N.Y. 11213
Tel. (718) 778-5436 • (718) 493-9250 • (718) 774-4000

ISBN 0-8266-0531-1

5753 • 1993

TIMELESS PATTERNS
IN TIME

CHASSIDIC INSIGHTS INTO
THE CYCLE OF THE JEWISH YEAR

Volume 1

Adapted from the Published Talks
of the Lubavitcher Rebbe Shlita

by Rabbi Eliyahu Touger

Edited by Uri Kaploun

TABLE OF CONTENTS

PUBLISHER'S FOREWORD

Time as a Spiral

Time is often conceived of as a linear sequence of events; each moment, although connected to the past, represents a new response to reality. In Jewish thought, however, time is seen as a spiral. Its forward progression is modulated by set patterns, recurring cycles that help determine the varying tone and pitch of our weeks, months, and years.

The dual nature of time is echoed in the Hebrew word for "year" — *shanah* (שָׁנָה), which is related semantically to the root meaning "repeat" (שנה), but also to the root meaning "change" (שנה). In other words, the cycle of recurring spiritual influences that constitutes a Jewish year is modified from year to year, as new dimensions of those spiritual influences are heard — familiar themes with novel rhythms.

Highlights Within the Cycle

Prominent within the annual cycle are the festivals and fast days prescribed by the Torah and by our Sages and Rabbis. On a practical level, these dates represent a departure from routine. Our holidays are days of joyful celebration, and they are also holy days, beckoning us to inner growth and development. Every holiday represents a different mode of spiritual expression, inspiring a different dimension of our bond with G-d.

Every holiday has a body and a soul. The commandments and customs of each holiday are its body; the breath of life is infused into this body by the soul of the holiday, the spiritual message it conveys.

Not Only History

Though all the Jewish holidays commemorate events in our national history, they enable us not only to recall these experiences, but also to relive them. At the same time every year, the very same spiritual forces which brought about the event commemorated by a holiday are again potently expressed. Thus the Fifteenth of Nissan, the date of our Exodus from Egypt, remains eternally "the season of our freedom," and the Tenth of Tishrei, the day on which G-d forgave the sin of the Golden Calf, is "the Day of Atonement" for all time.

The essays in these volumes are adaptations of the published talks of the Lubavitcher Rebbe *Shlita* which highlight the respective spiritual messages of the holidays. These essays are intended to show the connection between the historical significance of these days and their eternal relevance to our current divine service.

Holidays of the Future

We have also included essays on the spiritual significance of the communal fast days, for their observance too conveys messages of personal development. Recalling the spiritual deficiencies which brought about the calamities commemorated by these fasts is intended to inspire us to turn to G-d in *teshuvah,* to upgrade the content of our daily lives and the quality of our interpersonal contacts. Furthermore, these dates too will ultimately be festivals, for in the Era of the

Redemption, "all the [commemorative] fasts... will be transformed into holidays, and days of rejoicing and celebration."[1]

Chassidic Festivals

In 5662 (1901), the urgent communal needs of Russian
Jewry detained the Rebbe Rashab in Moscow. He was thus
unable to join his chassidim in Lubavitch in celebrating *Yud-
Tes* Kislev, the anniversary of Rabbi Shneur Zalman of Liadi's
liberation from prison. By way of compensation for his absence, he sent a historic letter[2] to his chassidim in which he
refers to *Yud-Tes* Kislev as "the Rosh HaShanah of *Chassidus.*"

The Rebbe's letter resounded not only among his followers,[3] but talk of it also spread beyond chassidic circles. A
certain scholar mentioned it to the celebrated halachic
authority, Rabbi Chaim Ozer Grodzinsky, and added mock-
ingly, "The *Mishnah* speaks of only four kinds of Rosh
HaShanah,[4] and now the chassidim have gone and added a
fifth...."

Reb Chaim Ozer replied: "They, at least, are constantly
growing."

Accordingly, this work includes essays on chassidic festivals celebrated in the Lubavitch community. However, the
potential for growth alluded to by Reb Chaim Ozer has led to
such a proliferation of chassidic holidays, that one can literally fulfill the verse,[5] "A good-hearted person is always celebrating." After careful consideration, it was decided to
include only four of the more prominent chassidic festivals:
Yud-Tes Kislev, *Yud* Shvat, *Yud-Beis* Tammuz, and *Chai* Elul.

---

1. *Rambam, Hilchos Taaniyos* 5:19; cf. *Rosh HaShanah* 18b.
2. An English translation of this letter appears in *Sefer HaMinhagim* (English edition;
   Kehot, N.Y., 1991), p. 153.
3. *Kuntres U'Maayon* (Hebrew edition only; Kehot, N.Y.), p. 25.
4. *Rosh HaShanah* 1:1.
5. *Mishlei* 15:15. Significantly, it is with this verse that the *Rama* chose to conclude
   his discussion of the festivals (in his Gloss to the *Shulchan Aruch, Orach Chayim,*
   sec. 697).

Patterns Within a Greater Cycle

Although each of the festivals conveys a unique message, the fragrance of each one lingers on and flavors those which follow, because they represent patterns within a greater cycle.

Like the cycle of the Jewish year, the composition of this text too synthesizes a variety of contributions, especially those of: Rabbi Eliyahu Touger, who skillfully adapted the texts from their Hebrew and Yiddish originals; Uri Kaploun, whose editorial expertise enhanced their presentation; Rabbi Aharon Leib Raskin, who supplied many of the references; Yosef Yitzchok Turner, who is responsible for the tasteful layout and typography; and Rabbi Yonah Avtzon, Director of Sichos In English, whose piloting and encouragement at every stage of the project transformed it from dream to reality.

In Anticipation of the Ultimate Celebration

In a discussion of the nature of time in his commentary on the Torah,[6] the *Ramban* sees all of history as culminating in the Era of Redemption, "the day which is only Sabbath and repose for all time."[7]

We also make mention of the Era of Redemption at the conclusion of every essay in this book. This is not merely a stylistic device in keeping with our Sages' advice[8] to conclude any work with a positive theme. Our decision to conclude with the theme of Redemption reflects the manner in which the Rebbe *Shlita* has concluded his talks throughout the years, particularly in recent years. And his evoking of the Redemption is not merely a figure of speech: all of his

6. In his commentary on *Bereishis* 2:3.
7. *Tamid* 7:4.
8. Cf. *Rama* in *Shulchan Aruch, Orach Chayim* 138:1.

endeavors are directed to precipitating the coming of *Mashiach*.

May the study of the present work further the fulfillment of that purpose, and hasten the coming of the time when G-d will "enable us to arrive at other festivals and holidays..., celebrating in the rebuilding of Your city and rejoicing in Your service,"[9] with the coming of the Redemption. May this take place in the immediate future.

Sichos In English

Chai Elul, (1993)
Birthday of the Baal Shem Tov (1698)
and the Alter Rebbe (1745)

---

9.   From the request which concludes the first half of the Pesach *Haggadah*.

IN DEDICATION

To the Lubavitcher Rebbe Shlita, who for 91 years has dedicated his life to making the Redemption a reality. May G-d grant him the health and well-being to see that mission to its conclusion, and may we and the entire Jewish people join in celebrating the Redemption in the immediate future.

Rosh HaShanah

AT ONE WITH THE KING

Adapted from *Likkutei Sichos,*
Vol. IV, Rosh HaShanah;
Vol. XIX, Sukkos

Head and Beginning

There is nothing arbitrary about a name given in the Holy
Tongue: the very letters that constitute such a name disclose
the intrinsic nature of the entity named.[1] The name of the
New Year festival, "Rosh HaShanah," literally means not
"beginning of the year," but "head of the year." I.e., the relationship of Rosh HaShanah to the other days of the year[2]
parallels the relationship of the head to the other organs of
the body.

There are three dimensions to the relationship between
the head and the body. First, the brain controls the functioning of the body as a whole, as well as that of its individual
organs. Second, the life-energy of all the organs is centered in
the brain, each of whose components is connected to one of
the organs. Finally, the brain is the seat of the power of
thought, the highest of human faculties.

Our divine service on Rosh HaShanah is characterized by
spiritual parallels to each of these three physical functions.

First, on Rosh HaShanah we resolve to advance in all
aspects of our Torah observance, and the resolutions under-

---

1. See *Tanya, Shaar HaYichud VehaEmunah,* ch. 1, and the sources given there. See
    also *Shaar HaGilgulim, Hakdamah* 23.
2. See *Likkutei Torah, Parshas Ki Savo,* p. 41c; *Ateres Rosh,* the beginning of *Shaar
    Rosh HaShanah.*

taken at this time influence the quality of our divine service throughout the coming year.

Second, with Rosh HaShanah we begin the Ten Days of *Teshuvah* (usually translated "repentance"; better: "return"). Since *teshuvah* comprises all the other *mitzvos*, it can atone for deficiencies in the observance of any of the *mitzvos*.

Finally, the divine service of Rosh HaShanah involves a level of absolute connection between man and G-d. Our Sages[3] teach that on Rosh HaShanah G-d asks man to "accept Me as King over you," and in fact the recognition of G-d's sovereignty is a major theme of the Rosh HaShanah service.[4] This act of recognition establishes a bond between the essence of man and the essence of G-d.

Three Levels of Connection

These three elements of Rosh HaShanah are related to three levels of connection with G-d.

(a) The first bond is established through Torah observance. Because G-d's will is manifest in the Torah and its *mitzvos*, by observing them we connect our thoughts, words and actions with Him.[5]

(b) There is, however, a second and deeper bond with G-d. For while it is true that observance of *mitzvos* establishes a connection with G-d, the conditions of this relationship presuppose that the individual is a separate entity who desires to connect to G-d through this observance. *Teshuvah*, by contrast, involves a bond which relates man to G-d directly, without the medium of *mitzvos*.

---

3. *Rosh HaShanah* 16a, 34b.
4. The first reason given by Rav Saadiah Gaon for the Sounding of the *Shofar* is that it echoes the sounding of trumpets at the coronation of a king (cf. Avudraham).
5. See *Tanya*, ch. 4.

Each of us shares a bond with G-d that is not at all dependent on our deeds. For this reason, even a person who has failed to establish a connection with G-d through *mitzvos* or who has obstructed that connection by his conduct, is still capable of feeling a desire to return to Him.[6]

A person's desire to return to G-d evokes a response from Him. Like a father who loves his children regardless of their conduct, G-d maintains a bond with us which continues even when our conduct appears to draw us away from Him. And when a person turns to G-d in *teshuvah,* this bond surfaces and makes its presence felt.

Since the connection to G-d established through *teshuvah* is deeper than that which is established through the observance of *mitzvos,* it can compensate for any deficiencies in our observance of the *mitzvos.* Nothing can block the expression of this deep connection we share with G-d.

(c) Nevertheless, despite the depth of the connection with G-d established through *teshuvah,* a certain distance remains between man and G-d. In fact, it is our feeling of separation from Him that motivates our desire to return to Him. By contrast, our willingness to accept G-d as King expresses the idea of man's absolute bond with G-d.[7] Man accepts G-d's sovereignty because he cannot conceive of any alternative; he cannot conceive of the possibility of living without a King.

(This understanding of the King-subject relationship also applies to G-d. G-d, so to speak, cannot conceive of being without subjects. It is for this reason that He turns to man and asks of him to "accept Me as King over you.")[8]

---

6. See *Likkutei Torah, Parshas Acharei,* p. 26c.
7. The essential nature of the bond between subject and king is reflected in the fact that each will sacrifice his life for the other, a phenomenon which is uncommon in other relationships.
8. The supremacy of the connection to G-d established through acceptance of His sovereignty helps clarify another point. Our Sages (*Rosh HaShanah* 18a) describe the Ten Days of Penitence as "the ten days between Rosh HaShanah and Yom Kip-

Accepting G-d's Sovereignty

Our Sages[9] teach that G-d tells man, "Accept My sovereignty and then accept My decrees." The connection with G-d which is established through observing the *mitzvos* ("My decrees") is only possible after His sovereignty has been established. Even *teshuvah* is possible only after G-d's sovereignty has been established. For the essence of *teshuvah* is regret over one's past conduct and a firm resolution to fulfill G-d's will in the future,[10] and this presupposes an existing subject-king relationship.

In our divine service on Rosh HaShanah, we therefore focus on the core of our relationship with G-d, the acceptance of His sovereignty, for this serves as the foundation both for our observance of *mitzvos* and for our ability to do *teshuvah*.

A Selfless Self

Why is our absolute bond with G-d established through the acceptance of His Kingship? The answer lies in realizing that deep down, underlying the varied peripheral facets of our personalities, the very core of our being is our divine soul, an "actual part of G-d from above."[11] Therefore, it is not free self-expression, "being ourselves," that expresses who we really are. Rather it is in the acceptance of G-d's sovereignty that our inner G-dly potential finds expression. By getting to

---

pur." There are, however, only seven days *between* Rosh HaShanah and Yom Kippur; the total of ten includes both Rosh HaShanah and Yom Kippur.

The above insight, however, resolves this difficulty. There is an essential dimension of Rosh HaShanah (the acceptance of G-d's sovereignty) and of Yom Kippur (see the essay entitled "At One with G-d") that surpasses the status of these days as "days of *teshuvah*." These are the beginning and end points intended by our Sages in the phrase "between Rosh HaShanah and Yom Kippur." In addition, as mentioned above, Rosh HaShanah and Yom Kippur are also "days of *teshuvah*." Thus there are ten days of *teshuvah* between the essential aspect of Rosh HaShanah and the essential aspect of Yom Kippur.

9. *Mechilta, Shmos* 20:3.
10. *Rambam, Mishneh Torah, Hilchos Teshuvah* 2:2; cf. *Iggeres HaTeshuvah*, ch. 1.
11. *Iyov* 31:2 as paraphrased in *Tanya*, ch. 2.

the core of our relationship with G-d, we give voice to the core of our own being, to that quintessential element that is most truly ourselves.

Thus when a person requests of G-d: "Reign over the entire world in Your glory,"[12] his request should be a deeply felt desire, not merely a superficial statement. Every aspect of our being — and the essence of our being — should be given over to G-d.

Our acceptance of G-d's Kingship on Rosh HaShanah hastens the ultimate expression of His Kingship that will take place in the Era of Redemption. For then "G-d will be King of the entire world; and on that day, He will be One and His Name will be One."[13] May this become manifest in the immediate future.

---

12. Rosh HaShanah liturgy.
13. *Zechariah* 14:9.

At One with G-d; At One with Our Fellow Man

Adapted from *Likkutei Sichos,*
Vol. IV, *Parshas Nitzavim;*
Vol. XIX, Sukkos

The Core of Our Being

On Rosh HaShanah, our divine service revolves around the acceptance of G-d as King. Throughout the year, we regard G-d's sovereignty as an established fact and we relate to Him through His edicts, the *mitzvos.* On Rosh HaShanah, however, we focus on the essence of our relationship with G-d, accepting His sovereignty in an act of homage that encompasses our entire existence. In making this commitment, the fundamental G-dly spark at the core of our being comes to the surface.[1]

This expression of our spiritual potential has an effect in the human realm as well as in our relationship with G-d. In paying homage to a mortal king, the most august of nobles and the humblest of subjects bow together; their joint act of submission efficiently levels them. By the same token, all Jews, regardless of their differing levels of understanding and self-refinement, are joined in the unifying act of accepting G-d's sovereignty.

The bond which unites different individuals extends beyond the shared act of homage. At the deep-seated level of the soul where man is one with G-d, there is no division between one man and another. Recognizing our unity with

---

1. See the above essay entitled "At One with the King."

G-d in the king-subject relationship thus reveals the internal unity which binds the entire Jewish people.

An Organic Whole

The unity of the Jewish people may be clearly pictured by means of the classic analogy with the functioning of the human body.[2] Although the body comprises organs of diverse structure and function, all these components operate together as a single living organism. By the same token, though the Jewish people is made up of numerous individuals, each with his own distinctive nature, it functions as a single, vibrant unit.

The unity of the human body is manifest in two ways. First, although the limbs and organs differ in form and function, they work in complementary harmony, each contributing a necessary element to the operation of the body. The feet, for example, provide the mobility through which the senses are exposed to a greater range of stimuli enabling the brain to collect and process information.

Secondly, the unity of the body is manifest by a collective consciousness of self, an "I". The various organs do not perceive themselves as independent, separate entities, but as parts of an organic whole. When a person stubs his toe, not only his foot feels the pain.

The collective Jewish body is also characterized by both these kinds of unity. The divergent qualities and personalities which characterize individual Jews are complementary. Even as we function as individuals, we are part of a greater collective entity to which our differences contribute.

Our awareness of this shared identity should affect the quality of our relationships with others. Every Jew has his

---

2. See the *Jerusalem Talmud, Nedarim* 9:4; *Likkutei Torah* of the *AriZal, Parshas Kedoshim, Taamei HaMitzvos; Likkutei Torah, Parshas Nitzavim.*

own unique potential and personality. When an individual sees himself and others as joined in a collective, he can appreciate the differentiating characteristics, seeing them as resources to be shared by all, not as sources of competition and strife.

Jewish unity is also manifested at a deeper level in the fundamental oneness of soul shared by every one of us. We each have a share in the unique "I" — not the "I" of our individual, subjective consciousness, but the true "I" of the G-dly potential that exists equally in all of us.

In Self and Above Self

Each of the above dimensions of unity has its own merits. At the first level, there are obvious differences between the various organs, i.e., between individual Jews; here the unity results not from an overshadowing of the parts, but from their interrelationship and interdependence. From this perspective, the unity of the second level, in which the body operates with a single consciousness, appears to be more complete.

The first level, however, is superior to the second in that it permits the possibility of unity even in a bodily sense. The unity of an overriding consciousness does not acknowledge the separateness of each part of the body. By contrast, the oneness which is a function of interrelationship and interdependence does not negate the individual part even while maintaining unity. By the same token, the Jewish people are united not only at the point in the soul which transcends each individual's existence. Our unity can be maintained even within the context of our separate identities. Even in the realm where we appear to be separate and distinct from one another — i.e., as we exist in the natural world — we are unified and share a commonalty.

Extending the Inner Bond

The two dimensions of unity are related. Because we share a single essence — the "part" of our souls which is "part" of G-d — we can be joined by bonds of oneness even as we function within our individual identities. However, only our day-to-day awareness of our shared identity and common purpose makes it possible for us to appreciate this essential, spiritual bond that we share.

Rosh HaShanah is (literally) "the head of the year," a time when we focus on the core of our relationships, both with G-d and with our fellow man. For this reason, the second, transcendent type of unity is highlighted at this time. Just as the head controls the functioning of the diverse limbs of the body, focusing on our inner unity on Rosh HaShanah leads to cooperation and common efforts throughout the days of the coming year.

The Key to Divine Blessings

Rosh HaShanah is a day of judgment, the time at which G-d determines our future in the year to come. By standing unified, together as one people, we bring about a year of blessings. As we say in our prayers,[3] "Bless us, our Father, all as one."

The Baal Shem Tov explains this concept[4] by likening G-d's relationship with the Jewish people to that of a father with many children. When is the father truly happy? — When he sees all of his children relating to one another lovingly. In the same way, the Baal Shem Tov explains, when G-d observes the unity of our people and perceives the bonds of genuine love that connect us together, His joy finds expression in abundant blessings for success in all our

---

3. The daily liturgy. As explained in *Tanya*, ch. 32, the very fact of being joined "together as one" makes us worthy of Divine blessings.
4. See *Sefer HaSichos 5700*, p. 157.

endeavors for the coming year. This, of course, includes the ultimate blessing, the coming of the Redemption. May it take place in the immediate future.

THE INNER MOTIVATION FOR PRAYER

Adapted from *Likkutei Sichos,*
Vol. XIX,
Rosh HaShanah and *Vav* Tishrei

The Paradox of Our Prayers

The *machzor* for Rosh HaShanah contains many prayers
which petition G-d that (for example) "we be remembered
and inscribed in the Book of life, blessing, peace and prosperity...." In addition to these communal prayers, many people
add personal requests for various material blessings.

Is it proper to pray for these things? Our Sages[1] teach that
on Rosh HaShanah G-d asks mankind to "proclaim Me as
King over you." In the midst of a mortal king's coronation,
what subject would dare approach his sovereign with a private request? Yet on Rosh HaShanah, while acknowledging
G-d's sovereignty, we also turn to Him with prayers for the
fulfillment of our material desires. This, despite the view of
the *Zohar*[2] that a person who makes such requests during the
Days of Awe resembles a parasitic leech crying, "Give, give!"

Still, these petitions are part of the liturgy for Rosh
HaShanah. The very same authority who instituted the
prayer, "Reign over the entire world in Your glory," also
included the request that G-d "inscribe us in the Book of
Life."

A similar paradox relates to the concept of prayer in general. In his discussion of prayer, the *Rambam* writes[3] that the

1.   *Rosh HaShanah* 16a, 34b.
2.   *Tikkunei Zohar* 22a, referring to *Mishlei* 30:15.
3.   *Mishneh Torah, Hilchos Tefillah* 1:1-2.

mitzvah to pray is derived from the Torah's commandment,[4] "And you shall serve Him with all your heart." Our Sages ask,[5] "Which is the service of the heart? — This is prayer." The *Rambam* goes on to say that "this commandment obligates every person to... petition [G-d] for all his needs."[6] How can asking G-d to provide for one's needs be called "service of the heart"?

On Rosh HaShanah this question is intensified, because Rosh HaShanah is "the head of the year," the time for renewing the core of our relationship with G-d. Since during this time we all pray more earnestly than usual, the content of our prayers is all the more significant.

Chanah's Prayer

The question of what to pray for can be answered by analyzing the story of Chanah the prophetess, which is the *Haftorah* recited on the first day of Rosh HaShanah.[7] Chanah had been childless for many years. Each year, she and her husband Elkanah would journey to the Sanctuary at Shiloh. One year, embittered by her barrenness, Chanah left the sacrificial feast, entered the Sanctuary and opened her heart in prayer for a son.[8]

> And it came to pass that as she prayed at length before G-d... only her lips moved, but her voice was not heard. And Eli thought her to be drunk.

---

4. *Devarim* 11:3.
5. *Sifri* commenting on the above verse; *Taanis* 2a.
6. See the discussion of this matter in the *maamar* entitled *Shoresh Mitzvas HaTefillah* in *Derech Mitzvosecha*, p. 115 ff.
7. *I Shmuel* 1:1-28, 2:1-10.
8. Significantly, according to the *Shelah* (*Maseches Rosh HaShanah* 214a), Chanah offered her prayer on Rosh HaShanah. *Yalkut Shimoni*, however, commenting on *I Shmuel* 1:3, gives the date as one of the Pilgrim Festivals. Our Sages derive several laws regarding prayer from the narrative of Chanah's prayer.

And Eli said to her, "How long will you be drunk? Put away your wine." "No, my lord," replied Chanah. "I am a woman of sorrowful spirit. I have not drunk wine or strong drink; I have poured out my soul before G-d..."

And Eli answered, "Go in peace. May the G-d of Israel grant your request...."[9]

Eli was the High Priest and the judge of the entire Jewish people. Considering his wisdom and experience, why did he immediately judge Chanah so harshly instead of trying to clarify the true nature of her feelings?

Furthermore, given that the *Tanach* does not usually dwell on negative matters,[10] why was Eli's error of judgment recorded for posterity? Finally, why was this particular narrative chosen as the *Haftorah* for Rosh HaShanah?

"I Poured Out My Soul"

In order to appreciate the significance of this narrative, we must understand that Eli never regarded Chanah as literally drunk; otherwise, he would have had her removed from the Sanctuary.

Eli heard Chanah's prayer and perceived her sincerity. When he accused her of drunkenness, he was speaking figuratively. He could not understand how Chanah — standing before G-d, in the holy Sanctuary — could think of herself and ask for a son. He considered her to be intoxicated by her personal desires, immoderately given to material things.

To this mistaken perception of her motivation, Chanah replied, "I am not drunk." (I.e., "I did not want anything for

---

9.   *I Shmuel* 1:12-17.
10. Cf. *Bava Basra* 123a: the Torah avoids offensive language even when referring to a non-kosher animal.

myself.") Rather, "I poured out my *soul* before G-d." (I.e., "My desire came from the very depths of my being.")

"Their Soul Longs Within"

Physical desires are not always motivated by selfishness. Although a person may think he wants material objects as ends in themselves, his desire may actually be rooted in the depths of his soul.

Everything in the world contains sparks of G-dliness which are concealed by the material nature of the world. Mankind has been given the task of refining the material and revealing its innate G-dliness. Every individual is destined to elevate certain sparks, and this divine service is necessary for his personal growth. If these G-dly energies are not elevated, that individual's soul remains incomplete.

The Baal Shem Tov expounded this concept in his inter-pretation[11] of the verse,[12] "Hungry and thirsty, their soul longs within." The Baal Shem Tov asks, "Why are they hungry and thirsty? — Because 'their soul longs within.' Their souls seek a bond with the G-dly energy contained in the food and drink."

We may be unaware of the spiritual motivation underly-ing our physical desires and consider them to be physiologi-cal, or psychological, finding all sorts of reasons to describe what we want and why we want it. In truth, however, a deeper driving force motivates our will. Why does a Jew want children, possessions, or material success? — Because his soul has an unarticulated desire to fulfill the G-dly purpose associated with these seemingly material blessings.

Hence Chanah's prayer. Chanah was not at all motivated by self-concern. This may be seen from her vow to dedicate

---

11. *Keser Shem Tov*, sec. 194, p. 25c; see also *Likkutei Sichos*, Vol. I, p. 177.
12. *Tehillim* 107:5.

her son "to G-d all the days of his life."[13] In "pour[ing] out
her soul before G-d," she did not express any self-centered
desire, but the inner motivation of her soul.

Accordingly, as soon as Eli heard Chanah's explanation
he responded with a blessing, asking that Chanah be granted
the opportunity to bring the innermost desire of her soul to
fruition.[14]

A Dwelling Among Mortals

With this understanding of Chanah's prayer, we can now
resolve the questions raised regarding the Rosh HaShanah
prayers. On Rosh HaShanah, we focus on the purpose of
creation — G-d's desire to have a dwelling place among mortals.[15] G-d does not seek sovereignty over spiritual beings, but
over mortal men who live their lives amid material concerns.

Man's desire for physical well-being may be seen as an
extension of his acceptance of G-d's sovereignty, not as a
negation of it. A person cannot serve G-d properly if he is
troubled by material concerns.[16] In order to continue his
efforts to construct a dwelling for G-d in this material world,
he asks for health and prosperity. These are not selfish
requests. Rather, his desire for material well-being is rooted
in G-d's desire for a dwelling place among mortals.[17]

---

13. *I Shmuel* 1:11.
14. This episode can teach us to judge our fellows favorably. A man who is moved
more deeply at *U'Nesaneh Tokef* (which speaks of material judgments) than at the
request that G-d "reign over the entire world in Your glory" (or at other prayers
which focus on spiritual matters) is not to be looked down upon. Realizing that his
prayer may well stem from the core of his soul we should pray, "May the G-d of
Israel grant your request!"
15. *Midrash Tanchuma, Parshas Bechukosai,* sec. 3; *Tanya,* chs. 33 and 36.
16. See *Rambam, Mishneh Torah, Hilchos De'os* 4:1; *Hilchos Teshuvah* 9:1.
17. Our requests for material blessings should, however, be accompanied by a process
of introspection which parallels the dialogue between Eli and Chanah. When a person prays, the "Eli" in him, the dimension of his soul which is a High Priest, must
ask, "How long will you be drunk? Why are your prayers so filled with personal

"May He Raise High the Standard of His Anointed"

The *Haftorah* of Rosh HaShanah rises to a crescendo with Chanah's second prayer — a jubilant outpouring of thanksgiving to G-d for having fulfilled her request. This second prayer concludes, "May He raise high the standard of His anointed" (lit., "...of His *Mashiach*").[18]

This concluding phrase is the point of connection between Chanah's two prayers, because in the Era of the Redemption, it will be openly manifest that the world is G-d's dwelling and that there is no conflict between the material and the spiritual.

From Chanah's first prayer, we learn that a person's desire for material things can reflect a spiritual commitment to divine service. From her second prayer, we see the ultimate direction and purpose of that service — the coming of the era when[19] "there will be neither famine nor war, neither envy nor competition, for good things will flow in abundance and all the delights will be as freely available as dust.... 'The world will be filled with the knowledge of G-d as the waters cover the ocean bed.'"[20] May this become manifest in the immediate future.

—

requests?" And he must focus on the spiritual purpose of his desire for material prosperity, so that he can reply as Chanah did, "I poured out my *soul* before G-d."
18. *I Shmuel* 2:10.
19. *Rambam, Mishneh Torah, Hilchos Melachim* 12:5.
20. *Yeshayahu* 11:9.

THE PURPOSE OF CREATION

Adapted from the *Sichos* of
Shabbos Parshas Nitzavim-Vayeilech, 5744;
the *Sichos* of *Erev* Rosh HaShanah, 5733

"Today the World was Born"

Rosh HaShanah recalls the creation of the world, as we see from the prayer,[1] "Today the world was born." According to our Sages,[2] however, the world was created on the 25th of Elul, so that Rosh HaShanah actually marks the sixth day of creation, the day on which G-d created man.

Why do we commemorate the creation of man and not the creation of the whole world? This is especially strange, given that the creation of the world demonstrates G-d's absolute power in His unique ability to create something from nothing.[3] Only G-d's essence, free of all limitation, can bring about being from utter void.[4]

The 25th of Elul, the first day of the world's existence, is further distinguished by being referred to in the Torah[5] as *yom echad* ("one day"), rather than *yom rishon* ("the first day"). The Torah thus indicates that on the first day of crea-

---

1. *Mussaf* service of Rosh HaShanah, based on *Rosh HaShanah* 27a.
2. *Vayikra Rabbah* 29:1; also *Pirkei deRabbi Eliezer* 8:1 and other sources.
3. *Ramban* on *Bereishis* 1:1.
    Creation of this nature took place only on the 25th of Elul. As *Rashi* (on *Bereishis* 1:14) explains, on the first day of existence G-d *created* the entire universe *ex nihilo,* bringing all the components of heaven and earth into being from absolute nothingness. On the following days, the days on which the Torah describes various entities as coming into being, G-d merely "formed" them, making new entities from existing substance by giving them distinct characteristics and locations.
4. Cf. *Tanya, Iggeres HaKodesh,* Epistle 20.
5. *Bereishis* 1:5.

tion, G-d was "alone in His world."[6] Though the entire created world already existed, it was not separate from its Creator; the world was one with G-d.

Conscious Acceptance of His Sovereignty

Despite its uniqueness, the 25th of Elul is eclipsed by Rosh HaShanah. This is because the creation of man opened up a new and deeper relationship between G-d and the created world.

Of all the beings in the physical and spiritual realms, man alone can choose to accept G-d's sovereignty. Only his relationship with G-d stems from conscious decision and free will.[7] Though G-d creates and regulates all the other beings in the universe, they do not consciously accept this relationship. Their link with G-d flows from G-d's creativity; it does not result from their own decision.

With the creation of man, G-d introduced the potential for voluntary acceptance of His unity and active consent to His will. Chassidic thought[8] illustrates the difference between G-d's relationship with man and His relationship with the remainder of creation by contrasting two forms of absolute rule, tyranny and sovereignty. A tyrant exercises dominion without his subjects' consent, by virtue of his might; the subjects of a king, even if he is an absolute ruler, may willingly accept his authority and seek his sovereignty.

Unlike every other created being, man has the choice of acquiescing to G-d's dominion or rebelling against it. He alone has been empowered to acknowledge the unity of G-d through his own thought processes, and to relate to Him as his sovereign.

6.   *Rashi, loc. cit.; Bereishis Rabbah* 83:8.
7.   See *Mishneh Torah, Hilchos Teshuvah,* ch. 5.
8.   *Likkutei Torah,* Rosh HaShanah, p. 55b ff.

Making G-d Part of Our World

Why must G-d's sovereignty be consciously perceived by man? From G-d's perspective, His unity with the world encompasses every facet of creation. Man is rarely able to conceive of G-d's unity from this perspective. Why, then, should mere man's awareness and recognition be of such importance?

Our Sages[9] teach that G-d created the world because He "desired a dwelling place in the lower worlds." In order for this desire to be completely realized, the establishment of a dwelling place requires not only that G-dly energy be extended into those lowly realms, but also that those realms be aware of the G-dliness in their midst and accept it. Only then is G-d's dwelling place in the lower worlds complete.

Before man's creation, G-dliness and the world appeared to be opposites; the world, from its own perspective, did not relate to the G-dly potential with which it is invested. Only with the creation of man did the possibility for an internalized awareness of G-d come into being.

G-d's Partner in Creation

Man was created not only for the purpose of expressing unity with G-d in his own life; he was also given the potential to suffuse the entire world with an awareness of G-d's unity. Adam, the first man, gave expression to this potential on the first day of his existence by addressing all of creation:[10] "Come, let us bow down; let us bend the knee before G-d our Maker."[11]

By imparting his superior relationship with G-d to the entire world, man becomes G-d's partner in creation[12] and

---

9. *Midrash Tanchuma, Parshas Bechukosai*, sec. 3; *Tanya*, chs. 33 and 36.
10. *Zohar* III, 107b.
11. *Tehillim* 95:6.
12. *Shabbos* 10a; see *Likkutei Sichos*, Vol. XV, p. 95 ff.

contributes a necessary element to the world's existence — a conscious union with G-d. This uniquely human perception of G-d's pervasive unity makes Rosh HaShanah, the day of man's creation, eclipse the 25th of Elul, for the potential for oneness with G-d that came into being with man's creation overshadowed all previous levels of creation.

Diverse Plateaus of Existence

The question, however, remains: Why do our Rosh HaShanah prayers proclaim that the world was formed on that date? Even if it is acknowledged that Rosh HaShanah takes precedence, it was on the 25th of Elul that the world was created.

This question can be answered by reference to a point of Talmudic law which relates to ritual purity. The laws of purity apply only to objects in a state of completion. For example, a shapeless piece of metal cannot become impure until it is fashioned into a useful object. Though the metal obviously exists, the laws of ritual purity do not yet relate to it; the object cannot be said to have come into being until it has been completed.[13]

Certain objects may be thought of as complete at any one of a number of stages. Animal hides, for example, can be used at one stage as covers or blankets, or they can be further treated and refined and made into clothing.

Imagine that a substance which imparts impurity comes into contact with a hide in a less developed state. Is the hide ritually impure (because it can be used as a cover at this stage), or pure (because it can be further processed into a garment)?

---

13. See *Mishneh Torah, Hilchos Kelim* 5:1.

The *Mishnah*[14] rules that the status of the hide is dependent upon its owner. If the owner would be expected to be content with the hide as a cover, the hide is impure. However, if the owner is a tanner who would ordinarily consider the hide to be unfinished at this stage and would be expected to further refine it in order to make a garment, it is pure.

This *halachah* lends us a conception of the status of creation before the advent of man. The 25th of Elul and the following days of creation revealed awesome G-dly powers. These powers were, however, totally eclipsed by the creation of man, which revealed a deeper purpose of creation and a higher aspect of G-dliness, just as the animal hide can be transformed into a garment by a skilled tanner.

The revelation occasioned by man's creation caused the world's prior existence to be considered unfinished. Through the creation of man, G-d established a new definition of existence, and according to this new definition, the world did not previously exist. The anniversary of man's creation can therefore be considered the anniversary of creation as a whole.

"As the Waters Cover the Ocean Bed"

The ultimate state of unity between G-d and the world will be expressed in the Era of the Redemption, when "the world will be filled with the knowledge of G-d as the waters cover the ocean bed."[15]

This will be accomplished through man's efforts. The revelation of G-dliness in the Era of the Redemption depends on our present endeavors to perceive and express the G-dliness invested within the world.[16] By developing a con-

---

14. *Kelim* 26:7-8.
15. *Yeshayahu* 11:9, quoted by the *Rambam* at the conclusion of his discussion of the Era of the Redemption in the *Mishneh Torah.*
16. *Tanya,* ch. 37.

scious bond with G-d and extending that relationship into every element of our existence, we bring closer the time when that connection will blossom forth into complete fulfillment in the Era of the Redemption. May this be realized in the immediate future.

The Fast of Gedaliah

THE LAST EMBERS OF JEWISH SOVEREIGNTY

Adapted from the *Sichos* of
Tzom Gedaliah 5747, 5749,
and 5752

"A Day of Divine Goodwill"

A fast day is described as "a day of Divine goodwill."[1] One reflection of G-d's favor is the Torah reading of the Thirteen Attributes of Mercy in the morning and afternoon services, for these attributes are a manifestation of unbounded Divine benevolence. Similarly, the positive nature of a fast day is demonstrated by the *Haftorah* in which we are told, "Seek G-d while He may be found, call Him when He is near."[2]

The positive influences of "a day of Divine goodwill" are especially manifest on the Fast of Gedaliah because it is observed during the Ten Days of *Teshuvah*. This period is the time at which the Thirteen Attributes of Mercy were revealed,[3] as alluded to in the verse, "Seek G-d while He may be found...."

Our Sages[4] offer two interpretations of this verse: In one, the verse is understood to refer to the Ten Days of *Teshuvah*, a time when G-d makes Himself especially accessible to man. The second interpretation links the verse to communal prayer. When a community prays together, the virtue of their unity causes G-d to draw close to man.

---

1.   *Yeshayahu* 58:5; see the explanation in *Tanya, Iggeres HaTeshuvah*, ch. 2.
2.   *Yeshayahu* 55:6.
3.   See *Zohar* II, 177a.
4.   *Ibid.*

Our Sages state that, during the Ten Days of *Teshuvah,* an individual's prayer can have the same power as communal prayer. When an entire community prays together during the Ten Days of *Teshuvah,* their prayers reach an even higher level.[5] By the same token, the positive influences of communal fasting are enhanced on the Fast of Gedaliah, because this fast is observed during the Ten Days of *Teshuvah.*

Aspiring to Redemption

The unbounded positive influence of a communal fast is linked to the era when goodness will spread throughout the world, the Era of the Redemption. This may be seen in the *Haftorah* recited on a fast day which concludes with prophecies to be fulfilled with Redemption, among them: "And My house will be called a house of prayer for all nations."[6]

In the Era of the Redemption, the positive aspects of the communal fasts will be revealed because all the [commemorative] fast days will then be nullified, and, ultimately, these days will be transformed[7] into days of rejoicing and celebration.[8]

The Fast of Gedaliah, in particular, is linked to the Era of the Redemption by the identity of the person for whom the fast is named, Gedaliah ben Achikam, the governor appointed by the Babylonians after their conquest of *Eretz Yisrael.* According to some opinions, Gedaliah stemmed from the

---

5. *Or HaTorah, Shir HaShirim,* p. 1462. This concept is alluded to in the use of the plural form of the word "seek" (דרשו). This can be interpreted to mean that "while G-d is to be found," i.e., during the Ten Days of *Teshuvah,* we should seek Him as a united community.

6. *Yeshayahu* 56:7.

7. The transformation of these communal fasts depends on *teshuvah,* which transforms evil into good.

    Teshuvah is not bounded by time. Therefore on the communal fasts, our people are able to atone for misdeeds committed in previous generations, even those, like the assassination of Gedaliah, which were carried out in the distant past.

8. *Rambam, Mishneh Torah,* the conclusion of *Hilchos Taaniyos,* based on *Zechariah* 8:19.

House of David[9] and was the last member of that royal family who commanded authority over *Eretz Yisrael*. This links this "day of Divine goodwill" with "the scion of David,"[10] *Mashiach*, who will restore the Davidic dynasty.[11]

The Fast of Gedaliah is also connected with the Redemption by virtue of the meaning of Gedaliah's name. The Hebrew letters of גדליהו[12] form the words גדול י-ה, "G-d is great." It is during the Era of the Redemption that G-d's greatness will be manifest throughout the world.[13]

The mention of Gedaliah in the name of the fast highlights the positive aspects of this day in yet another way. The other three fasts connected with the destruction of Jerusalem and the *Beis HaMikdash* are named by the Hebrew dates on which the respective calamities occurred. The name of this fast, however, recalls a righteous Jewish leader.

"May it Be Nullified Entirely"

There is another aspect of the Fast of Gedaliah that relates to the Era of the Redemption. This fast was instituted because the tragic assassination of Gedaliah extinguished the last embers of Jewish sovereignty in *Eretz Yisrael* after the destruction of the First *Beis HaMikdash*.

---

9. There are some indications that Gedaliah was related to the House of David, for it was a Babylonian custom to appoint relatives of the kings as governors. Even according to the authorities (*Radak* and *Abarbanel* to *II Melachim* 25:25), who state that Gedaliah was not related to the House of David, his murder shares a connection with that dynasty. Yishmael, the son of Nesanyah, was a descendant of the House of David. Jealous that Gedaliah and not he, had been appointed as governor, Yishmael murdered him. See *Sefer HaSichos*, 5751, p. 23.
10. Daily liturgy.
11. See *Rambam, Mishneh Torah, Hilchos Melachim* 11:1.
12. In *Yirmeyahu* and *II Melachim*, Gedaliah's name is sometimes written as Gedaliah (גדליה, e.g., *Yirmeyahu* 40:5) and other times as Gedalyahu (גדליהו, e.g., *Yirmeyahu* 40:11).
13. See *Rashi's* commentary to *Tehillim* 48:2.

According to many commentaries,[14] this actually took place on Rosh HaShanah. The commemoration of the tragedy was postponed, however, so as not to conflict with the festive celebration of Rosh HaShanah, a day when we should "partake of delicacies and drink sweet beverages."[15]

With regard to the postponement of a fast day, there is a Talmudic opinion [16] that "Once [the commemoration of a communal fast] has been postponed, it should be postponed [indefinitely, i.e., cancelled]." Understood literally, this statement expresses the minority opinion that when a communal fast falls on *Shabbos,* the observance of the fast should not merely be postponed until Sunday (which is the *halachah* as we practice it), but that there is no need to fast at all. However, the Hebrew wording of this expression leaves room for an extended interpretation, "Once it has been postponed, may it be utterly cancelled." I.e., a postponed fast is a time when there is a greater potential for bringing about the redemptive era during which the misfortunes recalled by the communal fasts will be nullified entirely.

The fact that the commemoration of the Fast of Gedaliah is always postponed,[17] indicates that this day is uniquely empowered to hasten the coming of the Era of the Redemption, when all the commemorative fasts will be transformed into "days of rejoicing and celebration." May this take place in the immediate future.

---

14. See the gloss of *Radak* to *Yirmeyahu* 40:1.
15. *Nechemiah* 8:10.
16. *Megillah* 5b. See *Likkutei Sichos*, Vol. XXXIII, the Seventeenth of Tammuz, 5748.
17. Moreover, Rosh HaShanah often falls on Thursday. In those years, the third of Tishrei, the day when the Fast of Gedaliah is usually commemorated, falls on *Shabbos,* and the fast is postponed further. Thus when the Fast of Gedaliah falls on *Shabbos,* the day is an even more potent catalyst for the Era of the Redemption.

The Ten Days of Teshuvah

TESHUVAH — RETURN, NOT REPENTANCE

Adapted from *Likkutei Sichos,*
Vol. II, *Shabbos Shuvah;*
Vol. V, *Parshas Lech Lecha*

Two Different Dynamics

The ten-day period beginning with Rosh HaShanah and climaxing on Yom Kippur is referred to as *Aseres Yemei Teshuvah* ("the Ten Days of *Teshuvah*").[1] At this time of year, our service of G-d is primarily directed toward *teshuvah.*

The conventional translation of *teshuvah* as "repentance" restricts its conception to one shared by Western society as a whole. The literal translation of *teshuvah* — and the conception expressed in our divine service — is "return".[2] A comparison of the meaning of these two terms through the eyes of the Jewish tradition reflects a radical contrast that sheds light on many aspects of our relationship with G-d.

Repentance implies a reversal of one's conduct — a recognition of past shortcomings, and a firm resolution to change in the future.[3] The two are interrelated; the awareness of our weaknesses impels us to reorient.

The concept of *teshuvah* as "return" emphasizes the fundamental spiritual potential of every person. Chassidic thought teaches that within each of us resides a Divine soul, a

---

1. Cf. *Rosh HaShanah* 18a.
2. Cf. *Likkutei Torah, Parshas Chukas,* p. 74a; *Parshas Haazinu,* p. 71c.
3. Cf. *Rambam, Mishneh Torah, Hilchos Teshuvah* 2:2.

spark of G-d.[4] This infinite G-dly potential represents the core of our souls, our genuine "I".

From this perspective, sin and evil are superficial elements that can never affect our fundamental nature. *Teshuvah* means rediscovering our true selves, establishing contact with this G-dly inner potential and making it the dominant influence in our lives. Seen in this light, our motivation to do *teshuvah* is not an awareness of our inadequacies, but rather a sensitivity to this infinite potential within our souls.

Returning With Joy

These two different understandings of *teshuvah* evoke divergent emotions. Repentance is generally associated with sadness, because feelings of regret and remorse play a leading role in prompting a person to change his conduct. *Teshuvah*, by contrast, is characterized by joy.

A *baal teshuvah*, one who actualizes his striving for *teshuvah*, naturally feels sorrow and remorse over his past mistakes. His dominant emotion, however, should be joy. For through *teshuvah*, he renews his connection to G-d and establishes a bond with his own spiritual potential. This, of necessity, gives rise to happiness. In fact, the absence of happiness indicates that a consummate connection has not been established and that more effort is necessary before one's *teshuvah* is complete.

Of Universal Relevance

Repentance appears to apply only to a limited range of people. Truly righteous individuals would appear to be beyond the need for repentance, while others might be con-

---

4.   Cf. *Tanya*, ch. 2.

sidered too completely estranged from G-d to be capable of this religious experience.

Defining *teshuvah* as "return", however, broadens the scope of its application. For if *teshuvah* involves gaining access to one's true spiritual potential, it applies to all Jews without exception. The same G-dly spark exists within the soul of every Jew from the most alienated to the most righteous. This Divine potential is infinite; no force or power can prevent its emergence and expression. Every Jew, regardless of his level, can therefore do *teshuvah*. No matter how low he has descended, there is nothing that can prevent him from reversing his conduct and establishing a bond with G-d.

By the same token, no one, not even the most righteous, is above *teshuvah*. Each of us, even the most spiritually developed, is limited by the very fact of his humanity. Our thoughts and our feelings, as well as our bodies and physical desires, reflect the limitations inherent in creation. *Teshuvah* allows us to rise above these limitations and establish contact with the unbounded potential of our G-dly essence. This, in turn, lifts the totality of our experience to a higher rung. Whatever our previous level of divine service, *teshuvah* can introduce us to a new and higher plane of spiritual awareness and capacity.

For this reason, our Sages teach[5] that "perfect *tzaddikim* (righteous men) cannot stand in the place of a *baal teshuvah*." For *teshuvah* reveals the infinite G-dly spark within our souls and connects us to G-d at a level above even the most sublime levels of divine service.[6]

---

5.   *Berachos* 34b, as cited by the *Rambam* (*Mishneh Torah, Hilchos Teshuvah* 7:4).

6.   This concept is connected with the coming of the Redemption, for the *Zohar* (III, 153b; see also *Likkutei Torah, Shir HaShirim*, p. 50b) teaches that *Mashiach* will motivate *tzaddikim* to turn to G-d in *teshuvah*. No matter how complete their divine service, the unbounded dimensions of G-dliness to be revealed in the Era of the Redemption will make them realize their limitations and will call forth a corresponding revelation of the infinite potential that their souls possess.

Recalculating Our Merits

Defining *teshuvah* as "return" rather than "repentance" also sheds light on the meaning of a problematic Talmudic passage. Our Sages[7] state that through *teshuvah,* all our past transgressions, even those committed intentionally, are transformed into merits.

We can appreciate that repentance erases all traces of the past, and that G-d forgives our sins and allows us to start anew. But how can repentance transform the sin itself, an act performed in defiance of G-d's will, into a positive deed? Sin *separates* a Jew from G-d.[8] How can it become part of a process of connection?

These questions are valid if we view *teshuvah* as repentance, an opportunity for a new beginning. When we conceive of *teshuvah* as a return to our true selves, however, these difficulties are resolved.

A Jew is never separate from G-d, even when he sins,[9] because the fundamental spiritual bond which links us to G-d is so strong that even when a conscious relationship appears to have been severed through sin, the inner connection is unaffected and continues to propel us toward *teshuvah.*

Distance Arouses Desire

Because our connection with G-d is always intact, sin, as an act of separation, may itself provide the impetus for our fundamental G-dly nature to surface. The feeling of being outwardly cut off from G-d may arouse a thirst for a more intense bond with Him.[10]

---

7. *Yoma* 86b; cf. *Tanya,* ch. 7.
8. Cf. *Yeshayahu* 59:2.
9. Cf. end of ch. 24 of *Tanya.*
10. Cf. *Tanya,* ch. 7.

Though every sinful act is a direct rebellion against G-d's desires, when considered as a phase in a progression leading to *teshuvah,* sin can be seen as a motivating force, directing a person to establish a deeper and more powerful relationship with G-d. In fact, the connection with G-d established through *teshuvah* is more profound and more intense than that experienced beforehand.[11]

All-Encompassing Oneness

Every element of our world exists for the fundamental purpose of revealing G-dliness.[12] Certain elements of creation reveal G-dliness overtly; other elements reveal G-d's Omnipresence indirectly. For example, the observance of *mitzvos* straightforwardly demonstrates that the material can be joined in a bond of oneness with G-d. The cycle of sin and *teshuvah* unfolds the ultimate truth of G-dliness, but in a different manner.

When a person first sins and then feels motivated to reject this behavior, these two steps, taken together, serve as a powerful affirmation of G-dliness, demonstrating that nothing, not even sin, can stand in the way of man's connection to

---

11. As stated above, "Perfect *tzaddikim* ('righteous men') cannot stand in the place of *baalei teshuvah.*" It goes without saying that one may not initiate a cycle of sin and *teshuvah* in order to attain this intense bond. As our Sages teach (*Yoma* 85a), "He who says, 'I will sin and I will repent,' is not granted the opportunity to repent."

    To borrow a term from our Sages (*Makkos* 7b), sin is "a descent for the sake of ascent." By nature, a Jew is above sin. Thus our Sages (*Avodah Zarah* 4b ff.) were able to state that certain sins "were not appropriate" to the Jewish people as a whole, or to particular individuals; they seemed to be out of character.

    Why, then, did these sinful acts take place? — Because G-d wanted to raise the people as a whole or the particular individuals involved to a higher level, and the only way this was possible was through their first undergoing the descent of sin.

    In this context, chassidic thought paraphrases *Tehillim* 66:5 and describes sin as "an awesome intrigue devised against man." When a person's *Yetzer HaRa* overcomes him and makes him sin, this is because it was prompted from Above to bring him to this act. Through this "awesome intrigue," G-d can bring man to the deeper and more intense bond that is established through *teshuvah*. (See the *Sichos* of *Shabbos Parshas Ki Sisa,* 5752.)

12. Cf. *Pirkei Avos* 6:11.

G-d. The sinner's act of return shows the infinite power of his G-dly soul, and reveals how it will overcome all obstacles in its natural drive for self-expression.

The unique bond with G-d established through *teshuvah* has repercussions far beyond an individual's personal sphere. As the *Rambam* states,[13] "Israel will be redeemed only through *teshuvah*. The Torah has promised that ultimately Israel will return towards the end of her exile, and immediately she will be redeemed." May this take place in the immediate future.

_____

13. *Mishneh Torah, Hilchos Teshuvah* 7:5; cf. *Sanhedrin 97b*.

Yom Kippur

TRANSFORMING EVIL

Adapted from *Likkutei Sichos,*
Vol. XIV,
Parshas Vayeilech

The Jewish Heart, "A Sanctuary in Microcosm"

A prominent element of the Yom Kippur service is the
Avodah, the poetic description of the tasks of the High Priest
in the *Beis HaMikdash* on Yom Kippur. Recounting the service in the *Beis HaMikdash* remains profoundly significant for
us, since the offering of a sacrifice was far more than a physical activity. Every activity carried out in the *Beis HaMikdash*
is paralleled within the spiritual sanctuary of every Jewish
heart. The physical procedure of offering a sacrifice, for
example, is an external manifestation of a certain process of
spiritual growth.

Although the sacrifices bore spiritual significance
throughout the year, their effect was heightened on Yom Kippur, when they were offered by the High Priest as the emis-
sary of the entire Jewish people.

The service performed by the High Priest comprised two
types of offerings: animal sacrifices offered in the courtyard of
the *Beis HaMikdash,* and the incense offering offered in the
Sanctuary. The Hebrew word for sacrifice, קרבן *(korban),* is
derived from the root קרב, meaning "close".[1] By offering a
sacrifice, a person draws close to G-d, elevating the natural
desires of his animalistic side and bringing them close to G-d.

---

1.   See *Sefer HaBahir,* sec. 109; *Sefer HaMaamarim 5709,* p. 29.

The incense offering, however, effects a deeper connection than that created by animal sacrifices. This is reflected in the Hebrew word for incense offering, קטרת (ketores), which is derived from the Aramaic root קטר, meaning "bond". Through the incense offering, a bond is forged, totally uniting man with G-d.

Reaching Down to the Lowest Levels

The animals used for the sacrifices in the Beis HaMikdash had to be kosher; i.e., the divine service of the animal sacrifices could elevate only those elements of creation which are by their nature fit for refinement. The incense offering, however, included musk, a fragrance derived from a non-kosher animal.[2] This indicates that the ketores could affect even those elements of creation that ordinarily cannot be connected to holiness.

Furthermore, among the spices included in the incense used for the ketores was chelbenah ("galbanum"). Our Sages[3] note that, in contrast to the other spices used for the offering, this spice has an unpleasant fragrance. It symbolizes the sinners among the Jewish people: they too are included in the bond with G-d established through the ketores offering.

In the same vein, the Zohar[4] explains that the incense offering was intended to destroy the impurity of the Yetzer HaRa ("the Evil Inclination"). The Sages of the Kabbalah[5] note that the ingredients used in the incense offerings total eleven, a number associated with the forces of evil.

---

2. This is the opinion of the Rambam (Mishneh Torah, Hilchos Klei HaMikdash 1:3). For precisely this reason the Raavad finds it unthinkable that a nonkosher substance should be used for the service in the Beis HaMikdash. In defense of the Rambam's position, it has been explained that the incense offering is an exception to the principle cited by the Raavad.
3. Kerisos 6b.
4. Zohar Chadash, commenting on Shir HaShirim 1:4.
5. Cf. Pri Etz Chayim, Shaar HaKaddishim, sec. 4; Torah Or, Toldos 20b.

A Day When Evil Has No Power

On Yom Kippur, the incense offering was of paramount importance. The spiritual climax of the day, the entry of the High Priest into the Holy of Holies, centered around this offering, which was therefore prepared with special care.[6]

The central role of the *ketores* in the divine service of Yom Kippur is, however, somewhat problematic. Noting the numerical equivalents of the various Hebrew letters according to the principles of *gematria*,[7] our Sages[8] explain that evil has no power on Yom Kippur. The numerical equivalent of the letters that constitute the word *HaSatan* (השטן), the Hebrew name for the angel of evil, is 364. There are 365 days in the year. On one day every year, Yom Kippur, Satan has no power.

Why, then, does the incense offering figure so prominently in the service of the *Beis HaMikdash* on the one day when the forces of evil are powerless? One might expect that since the purpose of the *ketores* was to negate the influence of man's Evil Inclination, this special emphasis would have been appropriate on any day *but* Yom Kippur.

Two Differences

This question can be answered by comparing the *ketores* of Yom Kippur and the *ketores* as it was offered on all the other days of the year.

On Yom Kippur, the omission of *maaleh ashan* (a smoke-producing herb) was punishable by death. While this herb also had to be added to the incense offering throughout the

---

6. Cf. *Kerisos* 6a.
7. *Shomer Emunim* (Dialogue I, sec. 21-23) and *Tanya* (*Shaar HaYichud VehaEmunah*, ch. 1) explain that numerical equivalence is no mere coincidence, but rather an expression of the inner life-force of the entities involved.
8. *Yoma* 20a.

year, if it was missing the punishment was not so extreme.[9] Furthermore, the incense offering of Yom Kippur was brought into the Holy of Holies,[10] instead of being offered on the Golden Altar in the adjoining chamber of the Sanctuary building, as it ordinarily was throughout the year.[11]

These differences reflect the differing spiritual goals of the two modes of incense offering. *Maaleh ashan* was included in the incense offering to ensure that the offering would produce a cloud of smoke. The ascent of the smoke symbolizes the refinement of the lowest elements of creation and their elevation to the highest levels.

On all other days of the year this herb was required, but not indispensable, since at that time the incense offering was intended merely to negate evil, not necessarily to transform it. On Yom Kippur, however, all elements of existence, even those on the lowest levels, are elevated and connected with G-dliness. It was therefore critical that the incense offering of Yom Kippur include *maaleh ashan,* whose rising smoke reflected this mode of spiritual service.

For the same reason, the Yom Kippur incense offering was brought into the Holy of Holies, the place where G-d's Infinite Presence was openly revealed. For only the infinity of G-d's essence can bring about a fundamental change in the nature of evil and transform it into a means of expressing G-dliness.

What is Our Motivation, Love or Fear?

Like all elements of the service in the *Beis HaMikdash,* the contrast between these two offerings reflects our own service

---

9.   This is the ruling of the *Rambam* (*Mishneh Torah, Hilchos Avodas Yom HaKippurim* 5:25). See the gloss of the *Mishneh LaMelech* to *Hilchos Klei HaMikdash* 2:3. Other authorities differ.

10.   *Vayikra* 16:12-13.

11.   *Shmos* 30:36.

of G-d: the two kinds of incense offering parallel two kinds of
teshuvah, that which is motivated by fear and that which is
motivated by love.

Teshuvah motivated by fear involves self-negation; though
the penitent may still feel an attachment to worldly tempta-
tions, he acts against his will to master his desires because of
his fear of G-d. By contrast, *teshuvah* which stems from love is
a process of self-transformation, whereby a person redefines
his basic identity. His striving changes *direction.* Instead of
being centered on fulfilling his own desires, he focuses on
cleaving to G-d and fulfilling *His* will.

The effects of these two forms of *teshuvah* differ. As a
result of *teshuvah* motivated by fear, "intentional sins become
like inadvertent transgressions."[12] As a result of *teshuvah*
motivated by love, "intentional sins become like merits."[12]

Why the difference? — *Teshuvah* undertaken out of fear
merely temporarily negates and overwhelms the power of
evil; it does not destroy it permanently. Though the individual experiences regret, he has not eradicated the problem.
Within his heart, he still desires the lures of the world, except
that he keeps them in check. G-d responds in a like manner,
withholding the consequences of his sins, but not obliterating
them entirely.

By contrast, the total transformation of self brought about
by *teshuvah* born of love evokes a corresponding reaction
from G-d. He transmutes our sins, acts of open rebellion
against Him, into positive merits.[13]

A Year of Blessing

During the year, the main impetus for *teshuvah* is fear. On
Yom Kippur, however, the holiness of the day affects every

---

12. *Yoma* 86b.
13. See previous essay entitled *"Teshuvah* — Return, not Repentance."

Jew: people feel a yearning to return to G-d and unite with Him. This feeling is an active expression of *teshuvah* stemming from love. In this way, our divine service on Yom Kippur parallels the effects produced by the service of the High Priest in the Holy of Holies.

When the High Priest completed his service in the Holy of Holies, he offered a short prayer, requesting G-d's blessings on behalf of the Jewish people. May our service on Yom Kippur also evoke G-d's blessings. May we be inscribed for a good and sweet year and may this year include the greatest blessing, the coming of the Redemption.

AT ONE WITH G-D

Adapted from *Likkutei Sichos,*
Vol. IV,
Yom Kippur

More than Absolution from Guilt

The name Yom Kippur means "Day of Atonement"; it is "the culmination of forgiveness and pardon for Israel."[1] The Hebrew term for "atonement" — *kapparah* (כפרה), implies not only that the sinner will not be punished for his transgressions, but also that the spiritual blemishes caused by sin will be washed away from his soul. When a person turns to G-d in sincere *teshuvah,* the process of change can purge, and even transform, the negative spiritual influences generated by sin.[2] It is, however, difficult to understand how can this be accomplished by the arrival of Yom Kippur on the calendar. How can Yom Kippur itself bring about such a dramatic change in a person's being?

The Essence of the Day Atones

This question lies at the heart of a difference of opinion among our Sages.[3] Rabbi Yehudah HaNasi maintains that atonement is granted on Yom Kippur whether or not a sinner repents, because "the essence of the day *(itzumo shel yom)* atones."[4] The majority of the Sages differ with this view,

---

1.   *Neilah* liturgy; *Rambam, Mishneh Torah, Hilchos Teshuvah* 2:7.
2.   See the previous essays entitled "*Teshuvah* — Return, not Repentance" and "Transforming Evil."
3.   *Shavuos* 13a.
4.   *Toras Kohanim,* commenting on *Vayikra* 16:30.

maintaining that Yom Kippur atones only for those who repent.[5]

However, even those Sages acknowledge the power of "the essence of the day," in their statement that on Yom Kippur we can atone for sins which cannot be completely atoned for on other days.[6] The difference between the Sages and Rabbi Yehudah HaNasi, then, is that the Sages maintain that "the essence of the day" can only affect an individual who through *teshuvah* has opened his heart to its influence. Rabbi Yehudah HaNasi, by contrast, maintains that the influence of "the essence of the day" is so powerful that it atones even without *teshuvah*. In order to understand this difference of opinion, we must analyze the nature of "the essence of the day" and how can it bring about an internal change within a person.

Three Levels of Connection

We relate with G-d at three levels.[7] The first level of connection is based on a person's Torah observance: his intellect grapples with Torah study, his emotions find expression in the love and fear of G-d, and his potential for activity is actualized in the performance of *mitzvos*.

The second level of connection is deeper than that which can be achieved through thought or word or deed. This bond surfaces even when the Torah-based connection to G-d has been severed. At this level, though sin may separate a person

---

5. This opinion is accepted as *halachah* (*Rambam, loc. cit.* 1:3, *Hilchos Shegagos* 3:10; *Shulchan Aruch HaRav* 607:16).
6. *Yoma* 86a; *Rambam, Hilchos Teshuvah* 1:3-4. Significantly, though the *Rambam* follows the opinion of the Sages, in the above *halachos* he quotes the expression, "the essence of the day atones."
7. See the above essay entitled "At One with the King."

from G-d, he will be inspired to turn to Him through the potential for *teshuvah*.[8]

Finally, there is a level of connection to G-d which stems from the fact that the essence of the Jewish soul is one with the essence of G-d. This bond is constant. At all times, our essence "cleaves to You."[9] This bond is not the result of our efforts, and consequently, neither our thoughts nor our words nor our deeds can weaken it.

Transcending Separation

The connection to G-d established through Torah observance is limited by the extent of each individual's religious commitment and actual observance. Furthermore, since this connection is humanly generated, it is limited, no matter how inspired and complete our observance is.

Even *teshuvah* — though it results in a deeper connection than that effected by observance — is limited, because it too requires human input: our yearning not to be separated from G-d.

The essential bond we share with G-d, however, does not depend on us at all, coming about instead, because our souls are "an actual part of G-d from above."[10] At this level of essential connection, there is no existence outside G-dliness, no possibility of separation from G-d, no possibility that the soul be affected by sin. The very revelation of this level of connection removes the blemishes which sin causes. This kind of cleansing is a natural process, for the revelation of one's inner bond renews our connection with G-d at all levels.

---

8. Similarly, this inner potential inspires a person who has not sinned to achieve a more powerful relationship with G-d.
9. The *Hoshanos* prayers of the third day of Sukkos.
10. *Iyov* 31:2, as paraphrased in *Tanya*, ch. 2.

When, by contrast, one atones for sin through *teshuvah,* the deeper connection he establishes breaks through the barriers he has created by his past conduct. Revealing one's innate inner bond with G-d is even more powerful: it leaves no possibility of imperfection.

This is the meaning of saying that "the essence of the day atones." On Yom Kippur, one's essential bond with G-d is revealed, and in the process, every element of our spiritual potential is revitalized.[11]

Locked In, Alone With G-d

The revelation of this essential bond on Yom Kippur is reflected in the High Priest's entry into the Holy of Holies, during which he came into direct contact with the Divine Presence. No human or spiritual being[12] was permitted to intrude upon his connection with G-d.

This same degree of connection can be achieved by each of us through our divine service on Yom Kippur, and in particular, during the concluding *Neilah* service. *Neilah* means "closing" or "locking". At this time, every individual Jew is locked in, alone with G-d. At this time, the essence of his soul, the level that is one with the essence of G-d, is revealed.

Neilah is the fifth prayer service of Yom Kippur. Our Sages explain[13] that there are five levels within the soul. The fifth and deepest is called *yechidah,* from the word *yachid* which means "singular oneness." This is the point in the soul

---

11. As explained in Note 8 to the above essay entitled "At One with the King," both Rosh HaShanah and Yom Kippur express an essential level of G-dliness that transcends their more general function as "days of *teshuvah.*"
12. *Jerusalem Talmud, Yoma* 1:5.
13. *Bereishis Rabbah* 14:9; *Etz Chayim, Shaar* 42, chs. 1-2. *On the Essence of the Teachings of Chassidus* (Kehot, N.Y., 5738) explains these five levels at length.

that is united in singular oneness with G-d; this is the level that surfaces during *Neilah*.[14]

The level of soul experienced during *Neilah* foreshadows the Era of the Redemption, for *Mashiach* represents the *yechidah* of all existence[15] and will reveal this unique connection in every aspect of our being. May this take place in the immediate future.

---

14. *Likkutei Torah, Parshas Pinchas,* p. 86b.
15. See the gloss of the *Ramaz* to *Zohar* II, 40b. See also *On the Essence of the Teachings of Chassidus.*

AFTER YOM KIPPUR: CAN WE MAINTAIN OUR CONNECTION WITH G-D?

Adapted from *Likkutei Sichos,*
Vol. III,
Parshas Acharei

The Morning after Yom Kippur

What should we feel on the day after Yom Kippur? On Yom Kippur, we naturally feel spiritually awakened, but what happens the following day? Can we sustain the heightened awareness of Yom Kippur throughout the year?

We find an answer to these questions in the Torah reading of Yom Kippur, which describes the sacrifices offered by the *Kohen Gadol* in the *Beis HaMikdash* on that holy day. The reading is introduced by the verse,[1] "And G-d spoke to Moshe *after* the death of the two sons of Aharon when they had come close to G-d and died." This verse teaches us a lesson regarding Yom Kippur — the importance of what happens afterwards.

Yom Kippur is a time when every Jew "comes close to G-d." That experience, however, must not be self-contained; it must be connected to the days and weeks that follow.

A Historical Precedent

In order to teach us how to approach this experience, the Torah recounts how Aharon's sons, Nadav and Avihu, made a fundamental error in the way they "came close to G-d" after

---

1. *Vayikra* 16:1.

the revelation of the Divine Presence at the consecration of the Sanctuary:[2] "Each took his fire pan, placed fire in them, and placed incense upon it; they offered before G-d an alien fire which He had not commanded them [to bring]. Fire came forth from before G-d and consumed them."

Although our Sages[3] enumerate several flaws in the conduct of Aharon's sons which led to their deaths, these interpretations raise a number of difficulties. Nadav and Avihu had been chosen by G-d to serve as priests. Moreover, as *Rashi* explains in his commentary on the Torah,[4] they had attained a higher spiritual level than Moshe Rabbeinu himself. How, then, could they have erred so seriously in their service of G-d?

Several Torah commentaries[5] explain that the death of Nadav and Avihu was not a punishment, but a natural consequence of their having soared to such spiritual heights that their souls could no longer remain in their bodies. Having experienced the rapture of cleaving to G-d in *dveikus*, they could not return to life on this material plane.

Spiritual Experience Should Not Be Insular

Even according to this interpretation, however, the conduct of Nadav and Avihu remains problematic because it was motivated by self-concern: they died because their souls wanted to cleave to G-d, to remain in a state of absolute unity with Him. In this desire, they lost sight of G-d's ultimate intention in creation. Like all the other beings in the physical and spiritual worlds, they too had been created so that G-d could have "a dwelling place in the lower worlds."[6] By leaving

2. *Ibid.* 10:1-2.
3. *Toras Kohanim* on *Vayikra* 16:1; *Vayikra Rabbah* 20:8.
4. In his comment on *Vayikra* 10:3, based on *Zevachim* 115b.
5. Among them *Or HaChayim* on *Vayikra* 16:1. See also the *maamar* beginning *Acharei* in *Sefer HaMaamarim 5649*, p. 237 ff.
6. *Midrash Tanchuma, Parshas Bechukosai*, sec. 3.

the world, even for the purpose of cleaving to G-d, they were thus in conflict with the intention with which G-d had created them and the world.

The deepest yearnings of our souls and the loftiest heights of our religious experience should be connected to the realities of our material existence. Spirituality is not an added dimension, separate from our everyday experience, but a medium through which to elevate our ordinary lives. By fusing our material and spiritual realities, we refine the world, infuse it with holiness, and transform it into a dwelling for G-d's Presence.

Entering in Peace to Depart in Peace

The goal of fusing the material and spiritual realms is clearly illustrated in the *Talmud*.[7] Four Sages "entered the *Pardes*" (lit., "Orchard"); i.e., they strolled amidst the lush profusion hidden in the depths of the Torah and experienced overwhelming mystical revelations. One of them "peered within and died"; another "peered within and lost his mind"; a third "cut down the saplings" (i.e., distorted by misinterpretation). Rabbi Akiva alone "entered in peace and departed in peace."

Rabbi Akiva was the only one who departed unharmed because he alone "entered in peace." He was not merely seeking mystical experiences. He did not enter the *Pardes* in order to satisfy a yearning to cleave to G-d, but in order to achieve a heightened spiritual awareness with which he could enhance his total service of G-d. His colleagues, by contrast, sought personal mystical experiences. They wanted to "come close to G-d," but did not understand how to relate that experience to the full scope of their lives.

---

7.   *Chagigah* 14b. See also the *maamar* beginning *Acharei*, cited above.

Extending Yom Kippur

The same potential problem exists with regard to our divine service on Yom Kippur. At the very time when we "draw close to G-d," we should not lose sight of our service of G-d throughout the year. Yom Kippur should not be viewed as an isolated experience, but as a means to enhance our relationship with G-d on a day-to-day level.[8]

The necessity of connecting Yom Kippur to the realities of the rest of the year is illustrated by the service of the High Priest on Yom Kippur. On this day he would enter the Holy of Holies where he was alone with the *Shechinah*, the revealed Divine Presence. No deeper religious experience is imaginable.

Immediately, however, he would offer a short and simple prayer, requesting blessings for an untroubled livelihood on behalf of the Jewish people.[9] Fresh from his ascent to great spiritual heights, he would immediately thrust himself into concern for the Jewish people on a day-to-day level.

Significantly, a prerequisite for serving as High Priest on Yom Kippur was marriage.[10] If the High Priest was unmarried, i.e., if he lacked this basic commitment to living within the practical realities of this world, he was considered unfit to intercede on behalf of his brethren.[11]

---

8. A similar concept is also alluded to in the Torah reading chosen for the afternoon service of Yom Kippur. By this time, for almost an entire day, we have — to borrow the expression of the Sages as cited in the *Shulchan Aruch HaRav* 410:9, 419:17 — conducted ourselves like angels. And what passage is read from the Torah at this time? — The passage (*Vayikra,* ch. 18) which warns us not to "imitate the ways of the land of Egypt, nor... the ways of the land of Canaan," and which proceeds to enumerate all the possible prohibitions against promiscuity. Of what relevance are these prohibitions to people whose conduct resembles that of angels?

   The answer lies in their possible relevance *after* Yom Kippur: observing this holy day is intended to influence our conduct throughout the coming new year.

9. *Yoma* 53b.
10. *Ibid.* 2a.
11. Here we also see a connection to the death of Aharon's sons. One of the reasons given by our Sages (*Vayikra Rabbah* 20:9) for their death was their refusal to marry

Fusing Spiritual Awareness with Material Prosperity

We, perhaps, do not experience the same heights as Aharon's sons or the High Priest in the Holy of Holies, but we do have spiritual peaks, times when we feel more in touch with our souls and with G-d. Surely this applies to Yom Kippur, a day on which we are removed from all worldly concerns. We cannot allow such moments to remain unconnected to our ordinary lives; rather, the spiritual power of these special days should be used to recharge our everyday service of G-d.[12]

This course of action also calls down blessings upon our material affairs. Yom Kippur is a day of judgment. When G-d sees that an individual focuses his intention on elevating the world around him and keeps that intention in mind even at the highest peaks of his spiritual experience, He rewards him with success both in his divine service and in his material affairs. G-d blesses him with health, wealth, and children. The individual, in turn, uses those blessings to elevate and refine the world, to transform it into a dwelling place for G-d.

This approach to the service of G-d leads to the ultimate fusion of material prosperity and spiritual growth which will take place in the Era of the Redemption. At that time,[13] "good things will flow in abundance and all the delights will be freely available as dust." Simultaneously, "the occupation of

---

and have children. This also reflected their desire for transcendence at the expense of involvement in the day-to-day realities of worldly experience.

12. As noted in the series of discourses entitled *VeKachah 5637*, ch. 96, our divine service immediately after Yom Kippur begins a new phase that can be described by the verse (*Bereishis* 32:2), "And Yaakov went on his way." As we complete our worship on Yom Kippur, we are reminded that the heightened awareness achieved should not be left behind as we proceed "on our way" into the humdrum daily world.

13. *Rambam, Hilchos Melachim* 12:5. In his *Hadran* on the *Mishneh Torah* in 5735 [adapted in English in the essay entitled "The Ultimate Good of the Era of the Redemption," which appears in *I Await His Coming Every Day* (Kehot, N.Y., 5751)], the Rebbe *Shlita* explains the interrelation between the material prosperity which will be present in the Era of the Redemption and the desire for the "knowledge of G-d" which will characterize that age.

the entire world will be solely to know G-d.... 'For the world will be filled with the knowledge of G-d as the waters cover the ocean bed.'"[14]

14. *Yeshayahu* 11:9.

Sukkos

THE ABILITY TO SEE HAPPINESS

Adapted from *Likkutei Sichos,*
Vol. II,
Sukkos

Two Offerings: Water and Wine

Our Sages state[1] that "he who has not witnessed the celebration of *Simchas Beis HaShoevah* has never seen happiness in his life." This refers to the celebration which accompanied the water libation, the offering of water in the *Beis HaMikdash* on Sukkos. During this unique celebration, the Sages "would dance...with lighted torches, singing songs and praises, and the Levites would play harps and lyres, cymbals and trumpets, and countless other musical instruments."[2]

In many respects, the water offering paralleled the wine offering that accompanied both the daily sacrifices and the additional *Mussaf* sacrifices offered on the holidays. In fact, the Torah's only allusion to the water offering appears in its description of the wine offering.[3] Nevertheless, no outstanding celebration marked any of the wine offerings, even though it is wine, not water, that figures prominently in the joy of so many festive occasions. Paradoxically, the Jewish people's greatest outpouring of joy was associated with the water offering, not with wine.

---

1.   *Sukkah* 51b.
2.   *Op. cit.,* 51a.
3.   *Rashi* on *Bamidbar* 29:18; *Taanis* 2b.

Limited and Unlimited Happiness

Based on the principle that we must thank G-d for all the pleasure we experience in this world, our Sages instituted the blessings recited before eating or drinking.[4] The Sages indicated the unique status of wine — the degree to which it gives pleasure — by composing a special blessing for it, *boreh pri hagefen*. In contrast, they did not regard water, which is tasteless, as sufficiently pleasure-inducing to warrant a blessing; only when a person drinks water to quench his thirst is a blessing required.[5]

Wine and water represent different approaches to our service of G-d. The Hebrew word *taam* (טעם) has two meanings, "taste" and "reason". Taste and reason are related because the comprehension of an intellectual idea produces palpable satisfaction, not unlike the pleasure derived from tasting good food.[6]

Because wine is pleasant-tasting it has come to symbolize the kind of divine service that is flavored by understanding.[7] Water, which is tasteless and simple, symbolizes *kabbalas ol*, the acceptance of the yoke of heaven — a simple commitment to fulfill G-d's will whether one understands or not.

Generally, we take pleasure from performing a *mitzvah* we understand, because this enables us to appreciate the positive effect produced by our efforts. By the same token, when we do not understand the reasons for a *mitzvah*, we may feel less fulfilled. Though we may be willing to obey G-d's will at all times, we do not usually derive as much pleasure from *mitzvos* which require our unquestioning acceptance.

There are times, however, when the approach of *kabbalas ol* generates a satisfaction deeper and more fulfilling than that

---

4.   *Berachos* 35a; *Rambam, Hilchos Berachos* 2:1.
5.   *Berachos* 44a.
6.   See *Kuntres Uma'ayon*, Discourse 1.
7.   See *Likkutei Torah*, Sukkos, p. 79d.

which is experienced from a rational service of G-d. When we are "thirsty", when we desire to be united with G-d in a way that transcends the limited scope of our thoughts and feelings, we derive pleasure from "water", from *kabbalas ol*.

At this level of commitment, the pleasure of fulfilling *mitzvos* through *kabbalas ol* exceeds the satisfaction of the rational approach, since the happiness produced through our understanding is, by definition, limited in proportion to our understanding. The more extensive our knowledge, the greater the pleasure we receive; where our knowledge is limited, so is our pleasure.

In contrast, the commitment of *kabbalas ol* that results from "thirst" results in a happiness that knows no bounds. For by making a commitment beyond the scope of our understanding, we connect with the infinite dimensions of G-dliness. This brings about a joy which entirely surpasses our human potential.

In Continuation of the Days of Awe

In this context, Sukkos and the water offering can be seen as a stage in the progressive divine service begun on Rosh HaShanah. On Rosh HaShanah and Yom Kippur we accept G-d's sovereignty and turn to Him in sincere *teshuvah*. These days challenge us to penetrate to our core and awaken within ourselves a "thirst" to enter into a deep, all-encompassing relationship with G-d. This "thirst" is satisfied through the service of *kabbalas ol* that is symbolized by the water offering.

The celebrations of Sukkos are an outgrowth of our soul-searching on Rosh HaShanah and Yom Kippur. Because we awaken a commitment to G-d that is unlimited, our celebrations are likewise unbounded.

A Timeless Relationship

Both the wine offerings and the water offering had to be brought during the daytime. However, while a wine offering offered at night was thereby invalidated, this restriction did not apply absolutely to the water offering; after the fact, it was acceptable even at night.[8]

Day and night are classic metaphors for states of revelation and concealment in our divine service. A rational commitment, which is symbolized by the wine offering, is relevant only "during the day," when one has a conscious awareness of G-dliness. Since a rational commitment fluctuates with the varying extent of each person's understanding, it grows weaker when one's awareness wanes. A commitment based on *kabbalas ol,* by contrast, weathers all seasons; it is not shaken, even when our understanding is weak.

Fusing Both Approaches

The unique significance of the water offering does not minimize the importance of the wine offering; both were required in the *Beis HaMikdash.* Similarly, in the personal sphere, each mode of divine service complements the other. While the basis of our service of G-d must be *kabbalas ol,* that simple and superrational commitment is enhanced and intensified by a conscious relationship with G-d.

A commitment to G-d which exists beyond the limits of our understanding is not sufficient. For our relationship with G-d to be complete, it should be internalized until it permeates and involves all of our faculties — and that includes our minds.

---

8.   The *Jerusalem Talmud,* Tractate *Sukkah* 4:7.

The Key to Happiness

Sukkos is "the time of our rejoicing," a week-long celebration that includes an entire cycle of time and influences all the weeks that follow, infusing joy and pleasure into every aspect of our service of G-d.

Though the *Beis HaMikdash* is destroyed, we can experience — at least in some measure — the happiness of *Simchas Beis HaShoevah* by commemorating the water offering with celebrations throughout the Sukkos holiday. Participating in these celebrations generates the potential for us to "see happiness" throughout the year to come.

This happiness will also include the ultimate celebrations of the Era of the Redemption. At that time the sacrificial service will be renewed, and with joyful hearts we will bring both the water and wine offerings in the *Beis HaMikdash*. May this take place in the immediate future.

THE UNITY OF OUR PEOPLE

Adapted from *Likkutei Sichos,*
Vol. II, Simchas Torah;
Vol. IV, Sukkos;
Vol. XIX, Sukkos

Four Species: Four Types of People

The holidays celebrated in the month of Tishrei are of comprehensive significance[1] and the symbolism associated with their distinctive *mitzvos* is broad in scope. In this context, the *Midrash*[2] explains that the *mitzvah* of the *lulav* and *esrog* symbolizes the intrinsic unity of the Jewish people. The fulfillment of this *mitzvah* requires us to hold together either fruit or branches from four different species of trees — the date palm *(lulav)*, the myrtle *(hadas)*, the willow *(aravos)*, and the citron *(esrog)*.

These four species are noticeably different from one another. The *esrog* has both a pleasant taste and a pleasant fragrance. The fruit of the tree from which the *lulav* is taken, the date, has a pleasant taste, but no fragrance. The myrtle has a pleasant fragrance but no taste, and the willow has neither fragrance nor pleasant taste.

Taste symbolizes Torah study, because understanding Torah gives us a concrete pleasure, similar to the sensation of

---

1.   For the Hebrew letters of the word Tishrei (תשרי) can be rearranged to form the word ראשית, meaning "head of" (*Baal HaTurim,* commenting on *Devarim* 11:12). This implies that just as the head controls the function of the entire body, so too, does the month of Tishrei have an effect on the entire year to come. [Regarding Rosh HaShanah as the "head of the year," see the above essay entitled "At One with the King"].
2.   *Vayikra Rabbah* 30:12.

experiencing a pleasing flavor. Smell symbolizes the fulfillment of *mitzvos,* because the quality which usually motivates us to fulfill the *mitzvos* is *kabbalas ol,* an unquestioning acceptance of the yoke of heaven. Since we often do not understand the reasons for the *mitzvos,* their observance may be less tangibly gratifying than Torah study is, in much the same way that smelling something is less palpably gratifying than tasting it.

An extension of this symbolism enables us to see each of the four species as representing a different type of individuals. The *esrog* represents a person who studies Torah and fulfills the *mitzvos,* the *lulav* represents one who studies Torah but does not perform *mitzvos,*[3] the myrtle represents one who fulfills *mitzvos* but does not study Torah, and the willow represents a Jew who neither studies Torah nor observes *mitzvos.*

Fulfillment Depends on One's Connection with His Fellow Man

The *mitzvah* of the *lulav* and *esrog* demonstrates that no individual can attain fulfillment unless he is willing to go beyond himself and join together with his fellow man. Even the *esrog,* the species which symbolizes both the virtues of Torah study and observance of the *mitzvos,* cannot be used for the *mitzvah* on Sukkos unless it is taken in hand and held together with the humble willow. By the same token, no mat-

---

3.   The *Midrash* obviously does not intend to imply that people in this category do not perform *mitzvos* at all. On the contrary, our Sages teach (end of Tractate *Chagigah*) that even "the sinners of Israel are as full of *mitzvos* as a pomegranate [is full of seeds]." The *Midrash* is speaking here of scholars who focus their divine service on excellence in Torah study and regard *mitzvos* merely as media necessary to achieve that goal, but otherwise without independent importance.

    The same applies to the categories of Jews represented by the willow and myrtle. There, too, the expressions "without taste" and/or "without fragrance" are not absolute, but imply that the area described is not the area of primary focus. After all, as quoted above, the very same Jew who is likened to the willow is also likened to the pomegranate.

ter how much we develop ourselves as individuals, we cannot reach our true potential without the help of others. The unity of our people as a whole is an indispensable ingredient in the growth and progress of every individual.

The concept of unity is so central to this *mitzvah* that it is reflected not only in the requirement of taking all four species together, but also in the characteristics of the individual components of the *mitzvah*. Our Sages[4] stipulate that a *lulav* may be used for the *mitzvah* only if its leaves are bound together. The only species of myrtle that may be used for the *mitzvah* is that which has successive rows of three leaves each. In each row, the three leaves must be level with each other, with no leaf significantly higher or lower than another.[5] The species of willow used also expresses the concept of unity, since it grows in bunches.[6]

Growing from Our Contact with Others

The motif of unity is also reflected in the *esrog*. Indeed, because the *esrog* represents a category of people whose potential for achievement is greater than that of others, its emphasis on unity must be greater.[7]

The *esrog* expresses the concept of unity by virtue of the fact that it grows on the tree for an entire calendar year,[8] and is exposed to all the seasonal variations and changes of climate. Not only does the *esrog* withstand all these influences, but it responds positively to them; each of these influences contributes to its growth.

---

4.   *Sukkah* 32a.
5.   *Ibid.* 32b.
6.   *Shabbos* 20a. See also the series of discourses entitled *VeKachah 5637*, ch. 87.
7.   The above series cites the *Sefer HaLikkutim LehaAriZal* which points out that the Hebrew word *esrog* (אתרג) is an acronym for the verse, אל תבואני רגל גאוה — "Let not a trace (lit., 'the foot') of pride come upon me" (*Tehillim* 36:12).
8.   *Sukkah* 35a.

We must learn from the *esrog,* and not merely tolerate people of all kinds, including those with characters and personalities very different from our own, but actually grow through contact with their divergent perspectives. As the *Mishnah*[9] teaches, "Who is wise? — One who learns from *every* man."

Stages in a Sequence

These expressions of unity on Sukkos[10] are related to the motif of unity in the holidays that directly precede it, Rosh HaShanah and Yom Kippur.[11] There is, however, a difference between the approach to unity of Sukkos and that of the Days of Awe.

During the Days of Awe, our awareness of unity stems from the unique spiritual experiences of those days, during which we all step beyond our individual selves and establish contact with the fundamental G-dly spark in our souls. At the level of soul where no separation exists between man and G-d, no difference exists between one man and another. On Rosh HaShanah and Yom Kippur we are thus able to pray together as a collective entity.

Despite the intensity of this experience, it has a drawback. Since the feeling of unity we experience on the Days of Awe stems from a level in our souls far above that of our ordinary, everyday thought processes, after the holidays have passed and we return to the realm of ordinary experience, we may revert to a feeling of separation. Sukkos teaches us that we must remain unified even at the level where a person's indi-

---

9. *Avos* 4:1.
10. The theme of unity is also emphasized by the *mitzvah* of *sukkah.* As our Sages teach (*Sukkah* 27b), "All of Israel are fit to dwell in a single *sukkah.*" (See the essay which follows.) However, while the *sukkah* highlights the collective nature of our people, the *mitzvah* of *lulav* and *esrog* relates this togetherness to each one of the individuals who comprise this collective.
11. See the above essay entitled "At One with G-d; At One with our Fellow Man."

vidual identity is taken into consideration, where one of us is an *esrog* and another, a willow. Although differences may exist with regard to our potentials and the degree to which we have developed them, we still stand united, bound together in one collective entity.[12]

The sequence of the holidays is vital. The all-pervasive experience of the Days of Awe and the essential awareness of unity that they evoke prepare us to for the lesson of unity taught by Sukkos. The intense spiritual service of the Days of Awe jolts us out of our self-consciousness and enables to reorient our values, so that we can relate to each of our fellow men as we ought.

A Joyous Bond of Oneness

This progression towards deeper unity reaches its peak on Simchas Torah, when the scholarly and the unlettered, the observant and the non-observant, Jews from every background and way of life, join together in exuberant dancing with the Torah scrolls. Personal differences that at other times would divide them, fade away.

This unity is given tangible expression by the custom of dancing on Simchas Torah in a circle. A circle has no beginning and no end and every point is equidistant from the center. On Simchas Torah we forget who is a "head" and who is a "tail". A common nucleus unites us all and fuses us into a collective identity.

While Sukkos teaches us that even as individuals we stand together as a unified people, Simchas Torah takes us even further. At this time we lose all consciousness of our individual identities: we step completely beyond ourselves. The experience of Simchas Torah is not, however, a return to the level of the Days of Awe, during which we transcend our

---

12. See the explanation of the second dimension of unity in the above essay.

individuality through a spiritual service, linking with others above the level of ordinary experience. For on Simchas Torah, the absolute bond of togetherness is revealed within ordinary material experience, in the midst of eating, drinking, and dancing.

These joyous bonds of unity will herald the coming of the time when "a great *congregation* will return here:"[13] we will return to *Eretz Yisrael* as one cohesive nation. At that time, as promised by the prophets, "they will be crowned by eternal joy."[14] May this take place in the immediate future.

---

13. *Yirmeyahu* 31:8.
14. *Yeshayahu* 35:10.

THE SUKKAH:
FEELING AT HOME AMIDST G-DLINESS

Adapted from *Likkutei Sichos,*
Vol. II, Sukkos;
Vol. XIX, Sukkos

To be Surrounded by a Mitzvah

The Torah commands,[1] "For seven days you shall dwell in *sukkos.*" In defining this *mitzvah,* our Sages state,[2] "You must live [in the *sukkah*] just as you live [in your home]." For the seven days of the holiday,[3] all of the daily routines of our life must be carried out in the *sukkah.* As our Sages explain:[4] "For all of these seven days, one should consider the *sukkah* as one's permanent dwelling, and one's home as temporary.... A person should eat, drink, relax... and study in the *sukkah.*"

Our Sages point out that[5] "the *mitzvos* were given for the sole purpose of refining the created beings": by observing a *mitzvah* a person elevates himself and his surrounding environment. Most *mitzvos* are focused only on limited aspects of our being and limited dimensions of our environment. When putting on *tefillin* one elevates one's head, heart,[6] and arm, as well as the actual leather artifacts involved. When, by contrast, a person lives in a *sukkah,* his entire body is enveloped

---

1. *Vayikra* 23:42.
2. *Sukkah* 28b.
3. In the Diaspora we are required to dwell in the *sukkah* on Shemini Atzeres as well, though a blessing is not recited when observing this *mitzvah.*
4. *Sukkah, loc. cit.*
5. *Bereishis Rabbah* 44:1.
6. The *tefillin* are placed on the head and on the biceps of the left arm facing the heart.

by the *mitzvah:* even the most mundane aspects of his life become means of connection[7] to G-d.

The message of the *mitzvah* of *sukkah* is not self-contained; it influences our conduct throughout the entire year to come. The Torah simply tells us to[8] "know Him in all your ways"; and our Sages comment,[9] "This is a short verse upon which all the fundamentals of the Torah depend." For G-dliness is present not merely in the synagogue or in the house of study, but in every dimension and corner of our lives. This concept is made tangible by the *mitzvah* of dwelling in a *sukkah.*

Infusing Spirituality into Our Material World

Whenever one fulfills a *mitzvah* with material objects, a connection is established between them and the spiritual import of the *mitzvah.*[10] From that time on, they are known as *tashmishei mitzvah* ("objects used for a *mitzvah*"). Since their connection with spirituality remains, an object that has been used in performing a *mitzvah* should not later be used for unrefined purposes.[11]

There is an even deeper connection between the building materials used for the *sukkah* and the spiritual influences associated with it. Thus our Sages say,[12] "Just as the sacrifices become consecrated for the sake of heaven,... so too, the *sukkah* becomes consecrated for the sake of heaven."[13]

---

7. The Hebrew word *mitzvah* ("commandment") is related to the Hebrew/Aramaic word *tzavta* ("connection"). By observing a *mitzvah*, one establishes a connection with the One who gave the command. See *Likkutei Torah, Parshas Bechukosai* 45c.
8. *Mishlei* 3:6.
9. *Berachos* 63b.
10. See the essay in Vol. II entitled "What Happened at Sinai?"
11. Cf. *Megillah* 26b; *Shulchan Aruch, Orach Chayim* 21:1.
12. *Sukkah* 9a, quoted in *Shulchan Aruch HaRav* 638:1.
13. For this reason we are forbidden to use the building materials of the *sukkah* for mundane purposes during the holiday (*Shulchan Aruch HaRav* 638:15-16).

The *sukkah* represents a deeper fusion between materiality and spirituality than that which is achieved through the performance of many other *mitzvos*. In most instances, the connection between the material object and the spiritual effect established through the observance of a *mitzvah* does not permeate the material entity entirely. Therefore, though we are required to treat them with respect, these objects are not considered holy: they are not totally united with spirituality. Consecration implies that the physical entity becomes suffused with holiness, and this deeper bond is achieved through the *mitzvah* of dwelling in the *sukkah*.

"Your Sukkah of Peace"

Our Sages associate the *mitzvah* of *sukkah* with unity, as may be seen by the phrase,[14] "Your *sukkah* of peace," and in our Sages' statement that[15] "All Israel are fit to dwell in one *sukkah*."

Why is the *sukkah* associated with peace and unity? Chassidic thought[16] explains that observing the *mitzvah* of *sukkah* draws down to this world a transcendent spiritual light whose revelation erases all differences between men and establishes a fundamental equality among them. Our world is characterized by differentiation. The *mitzvah* of *sukkah* is intended to suffuse the world with a G-dly state of oneness that is, essentially, uncharacteristic of this diverse world.

In another sense, the unity established by this *mitzvah* resolves the differences that exist between spirituality and material existence. From the perspective of the world, the two appear to be opposites. From G-d's perspective, however, both the material and the spiritual are expressions of Himself and can be fused together harmoniously.

---

14. Daily liturgy.
15. *Sukkah* 27b.
16. See the series of discourses entitled *VeKachah 5637*, chs. 95-96.

The Ultimate Sukkah

Our Rabbis[17] explain that through dwelling in the *sukkah* we will merit the rebuilding of the *Beis HaMikdash,* as is implied by the verse,[18] "And His *sukkah* will be in [Jeru]salem." The ultimate fusion between the material and the spiritual will take place in the Era of the Redemption and in particular, in the *Beis HaMikdash,* where the Divine Presence will be openly revealed. May this take place in the immediate future.

---

17. *Maharsha,* commenting on *Pesachim* 5a. See also the *Targum* and *Midrash Tehillim* to *Tehillim* 76:3.
18. *Tehillim* 76:3.

WE DO NOT REJOICE ALONE

Adapted from
MiMaayenei HaYeshuah,
sec. 3

Our Sukkos Guests

We refer to our festivals as "festivals for rejoicing, holidays and seasons for gladness."[1] A happy person naturally wants to share his joy with others. Inner satisfaction may be felt alone, but exuberant celebration can be experienced only in the company of others. As an expression of our happiness, our Rabbis stressed the importance of sharing the joy of the festivals by inviting guests to our holiday meals.[2] This *mitzvah* is especially important on Sukkos, "the season of our rejoicing."[3]

The *Zohar* teaches that our Sukkos guests include not only those who visibly partake of the festive meals, but also guests from the spiritual realm. On Sukkos we are joined in the *sukkah* by seven *Ushpizin* ("honored guests"): Avraham, Yitzchak, Yaakov, Moshe, Aharon, Yosef, and King David.[4]

---

1. Holiday liturgy.
2. See *Rambam, Mishneh Torah, Hilchos Shvisas Yom-Tov* 6:18, where inviting guests is described as the ultimate expression of the rejoicing associated with a festival.
3. Holiday liturgy. See also *Yalkut Shimoni, Parshas Emor,* sec. 654.
4. The above series follows the order given in the *Zohar* (III, 103b), which enumerates the *Ushpizin* according to the sequence of the *Sefiros* which they represent. Elsewhere, significantly, the *Zohar* (I, 261a) enumerates the *Ushpizin* in chronological order. In a third place (III, 255a), the *Zohar* substitutes King Shlomo for Yosef. In regard to differences of opinion among our Sages we find the expression (*Eruvin* 13b), "These *and* these are the words of the living G-d." Hence, though our discussion of the *Ushpizin* follows the order of the *Sefiros,* all of these perspectives are relevant to one's divine service.

In addition, the Previous Rebbe taught that our *sukkos* are also visited by chassidic *Ushpizin*. In fact, he would actually point to particular places in his *sukkah* and say,[5] "Here sits the Baal Shem Tov; here, the Maggid of Mezritch; here, the Alter Rebbe; here, the Mitteler Rebbe; here, the *Tzemach Tzedek;* here, the Rebbe Maharash; and here, the Rebbe Rashab."

Although these *Ushpizin* visit our *sukkos* together on every day of the holiday, on each of the days of Sukkos the influence of one of the *Ushpizin* is dominant,[6] and his qualities teach us lessons to apply in our service of G-d.

The Guests of the First Day: Avraham Avinu and the Baal Shem Tov

The *Ushpizin* of the first day, the Patriarch Avraham and the Baal Shem Tov, share certain characteristics. Each of them initiated a new stage in the relationship between man and G-d. Avraham was the founder of the Jewish faith, and the Baal Shem Tov, of the chassidic movement. Furthermore, both Avraham and the Baal Shem Tov traveled from place to place in order to reveal G-d's presence within the world.

On the verse,[7] "And he called *(vayikra)* upon the name of G-d, the eternal L-rd," our Sages[8] comment, "Do not read *vayikra* ('and he called') but *vayakri* ('and he caused others to call...'), for Avraham made all the wayfarers [he encountered] call upon the name of G-d."

Chassidic thought[9] notes that the Hebrew word *olam* in the above phrase עולם א-ל ("eternal L-rd") means both

---

5. See *Sefer HaSichos 5697*, p. 161, and the *Sichos* of the first night of Sukkos, 5703.
6. This is indicated by the invitation traditionally extended to the *Ushpizin:* "May .... enter, and with him...." Although it is not Lubavitch custom to recite this invitation, we can derive lessons in our divine service from it.
7. *Bereishis* 21:33.
8. *Sotah* 10a.
9. *Likkutei Torah, Parshas Ki Savo*, p. 42d.

"eternal" and also "world". Since Avraham revealed the complete unity between G-d and the world, the verse does not use the phrase א-ל העולם ("L-rd *of* the world"), which would imply that the world is a separate entity over which G-d rules, but rather, א-ל עולם, which implies that the two are fused in perfect unity.

Like our father Avraham, the Baal Shem Tov sought out the common people. He would ask them about their health, jobs, and other material concerns in order to elicit the grateful response, *Baruch HaShem* ("Blessed be G-d!"). In doing so, he demonstrated that G-dliness is part of even the most mundane dimensions of our existence.[10]

The Guests of the Second Day: Yitzchak Avinu and the Maggid of Mezritch

The characteristic shared by these two *Ushpizin* is alluded to by the verse,[11] "Do not abandon your place." In contrast to the other Patriarchs, Yitzchak never left *Eretz Yisrael*. Similarly, in contrast to the other Rebbeim who journeyed from place to place, the Maggid never left Mezritch after assuming leadership of the chassidic movement.[12]

The essence of every person is his G-dly core. This, and not any geographical location, is every person's true place and that which defines his being. The Patriarch Yitzchak and the Maggid of Mezritch taught that one should focus on penetrating to this core and bringing it to the surface, instead of seeking to grow from outside influences.[13] Thus, the Torah

---

10. *Sefer HaMaamarim — Yiddish*, p. 138 ff.
11. *Koheles* 10:4.
12. See *HaYom Yom*, entry for 3 Kislev.
13. This concept obviously does not negate the value of traveling as a valid means of refreshing one's divine service. Nevertheless, on the second day of Sukkos we emphasize the approach to divine service exemplified by the *Ushpizin* of that day.

describes Yitzchak as digging wells,[14] searching for the source of flowing water and allowing it to surface.

Focusing on one's own place does not diminish the significance of others. Chassidic thought explains[15] that the revelation of a powerful light has an elevating influence even on far-removed places. For example, the light of the *Beis HaMikdash* was diffused throughout the world, spreading holiness to the extent that people in distant places, such as the Queen of Sheba,[16] were motivated to journey to Jerusalem.

The Guests of the Third Day: Yaakov Avinu and the Alter Rebbe

Both *Ushpizin* of the third day are especially associated with Torah study. The Torah[17] describes Yaakov as "a simple man, dwelling in tents," which our Sages understand as a reference to "the tents of Shem and Eiver,"[18] the leading houses of study of that age.

The Alter Rebbe's connection to Torah study is hinted at in his first name, Shneur, which can be read as *shnei or* ("two lights"), in allusion to the light of *nigleh,* the revealed dimension of Torah law, and *pnimiyus HaTorah,* the hidden, mystical dimension of the Torah.[19] These two modes of spiritual illumination shine forth in the Alter Rebbe's two classics, the *Shulchan Aruch* and the *Tanya.*[20]

Everyone has his share in the Torah, and this connection should be expressed in our daily conduct. Thus, our Sages teach,[21] "[The example of] Hillel obligates the poor and [the

---

14. See *Bereishis,* ch. 26.
15. *Torah Or, Parshas Bereishis* 6a.
16. See *I Melachim,* ch. 10.
17. *Bereishis* 25:27.
18. *Bereishis Rabbah* 63:10, and *Rashi* on the verse cited.
19. As explained in *Or HaTorah,* Vol. 1, commenting on the above verse.
20. See *Beis Rebbe,* Vol. I, ch. 25, note 10; *Likkutei Sichos,* Vol. VI, p. 37.
21. *Yoma* 35b.

example of] Rabbi Elazar ben Charsom obligates the rich [to study Torah]." Although Hillel was a poor man who labored hard for his livelihood, he studied Torah diligently, while Rabbi Elazar ben Charsom, who was extremely wealthy, did not allow his thriving business concerns to divert his attention from Torah study. Regardless of one's financial status, everyone has both the potential and the responsibility to devote himself to the study of the Torah.

The Guests of the Fourth Day: Moshe Rabbeinu and the Mitteler Rebbe

The *Ushpizin* of the fourth day are also associated with Torah study. Moshe "received the Torah from Sinai and transmitted it" to the entire Jewish people.[22] Indeed, the Torah is associated with his name to the extent that the prophets[23] refer to it as "the Torah of Moshe, My servant."

Moshe's connection to the Torah was twofold: (a) he served as the intermediary who communicated the Torah to the Jewish people; (b) he interpreted the Torah, developing the approach of abstract argumentation within Torah law which is referred to as *pilpula de'oraysa*. Significantly, he also sought to communicate this dimension of Torah to others.[24]

Like Moshe Rabbeinu, the Mitteler Rebbe served as both transmitter and interpreter, for the Mitteler Rebbe was renowned for his detailed explanation of the philosophical concepts of *Chassidus*. While the Alter Rebbe laid the foundation for an understanding of chassidic thought, he revealed his ideas as essential points, flashes of lightning.[25] The

---

22. *Avos* 1:1.
23. *Malachi* 3:22.
24. Cf. *Nedarim* 38a.
25. The Alter Rebbe is identified with the *Sefirah* of *Chochmah* (lit., "wisdom"), which is expressed as a flash of seminal intuition. The Mitteler Rebbe, by contrast, is identified with the *Sefirah* of *Binah* (lit., "understanding"), whose detailed analysis and explanation make it resemble intellectual gestation. See *Sefer HaSichos 5696*, p. 141.

Mitteler Rebbe amplified these ideas, explaining them with examples and analogies, and developing a conceptual framework which allowed them to be internalized — grasped intellectually.

Though the *Ushpizin* of the third day are also connected with Torah study, those of the fourth day, Moshe Rabbeinu and the Mitteler Rebbe, show how our Torah study can be amplified. Their divine service demonstrates that everyone shares a connection not only with the fundamentals of Torah study, but also with a comprehension of its depth and breadth. And with regard to this dimension as well, neither poverty nor wealth can excuse one from the responsibility of applying oneself to this task.

The Guests of the Fifth Day: Aharon HaKohen and the Tzemach Tzedek

The *Ushpizin* of the fifth day teach a lesson of love and harmony among all men. Aharon is the epitome of this approach, because he "loved peace, pursued peace, loved created beings, and drew them near to the Torah."[26]

The use of the term "created beings" instead of "people" implies that Aharon would reach out to individuals whose only redeeming virtue was the fact that they were G-d's creations.[27] Aharon's concern for his fellow man was all the more impressive because of his exalted position as High Priest. Leaving the Sanctuary where G-d's presence was openly revealed to him, he would reach out to people who had no other virtue than being created by G-d.[28]

---

26. *Avos* 1:12.
27. *Tanya*, ch. 32.
28. There is an added dimension of self-sacrifice to Aharon's conduct. While outside the Sanctuary dealing with people on this level he could easily contract ritual impurity, which would require him to remain outside the Sanctuary for even a longer period. Nevertheless, he was willing to take this risk in the cause of spreading brotherly love.

Also significant is the phrase, "drew them near to the Torah." This implies that Aharon first concerned himself with the difficulties that confronted them,[29] in the hope that ultimately, this would "draw them close to the Torah."[30]

The *Tzemach Tzedek* represents the development of harmony among the scholars and leaders of the Jewish community. Under his leadership, unity was established between chassidim and other sectors of the Jewish community. The *Tzemach Tzedek* met with the leaders of all contemporary factions and was able to develop a united front that emphasized the mutual purpose shared by all.

The Guests of the Sixth Day: Yosef HaTzaddik and the Rebbe Maharash

The qualities shared by the *Ushpizin* of the sixth day are expressed by a renowned adage of the Rebbe Maharash,[31] *Lechat'chilah ariber:* "People say, 'If you can't crawl under, try to climb over.' And *I* say, 'From the outset, climb right over the top!'" Apparent difficulties are waiting to be taken confidently by the horns and overcome.[32]

This is not a theoretical concept, but a truth that can be practically applied — as witness the life of Yosef, who rose from imprisoned slave to viceroy of Egypt.

---

29. Significantly, we find the same pattern followed by the Baal Shem Tov at the birth of the chassidic movement. First he became involved with the people's material needs, seeking to provide them with means of making a livelihood. Only then did he begin to reveal the teachings of *Chassidus.* See *HaTamim,* Issue 2, p. 44.
30. Though Aharon reached out to these individuals and tried to accommodate them to the fullest degree possible, his efforts were centered on "drawing them near *to the Torah,*" and not (G-d forbid) drawing the Torah near *to them.* His willingness to extend himself involved no compromise of principle.
31. *Igros Kodesh* (Letters) of the Rebbe Rayatz, Vol. I, p. 617.
32. It goes without saying that ambition and confidence should not stem from egotism. After all, "It is G-d, your L-rd, Who gives you the strength to succeed" (*Devarim* 8:18).

The lessons of Yosef's life are relevant to everyone. Though we are in exile, no individual should feel hampered or handicapped. We have the potential for the highest levels of achievement in spiritual matters, and this spiritual success may even be reflected in the advancement of our material concerns.[33]

The Guests of the Seventh Day: King David and the Rebbe Rashab

The attribute shared by the *Ushpizin* of the seventh day is royalty, the ultimate expression of which will come in the Era of the Redemption. King David is particularly identified with royalty, for "once David was anointed, he acquired the crown of kingship, which [thereafter] belongs to him and his male descendants forever."[34] Similarly, King David is identified with the ultimate monarch, the *Mashiach,* who will be one of his descendants. Furthermore, as the *Rambam*[35] points out, the prophecies in the Torah[36] which allude to the coming of *Mashiach,* speak about two anointed kings, David and the *Mashiach.*

These qualities are shared by the Rebbe Rashab, as is hinted at in the name of the year in which he was born — 5621 (כתר"א). These Hebrew letters spell the Aramaic word *kisra* ("crown"),[37] the symbol which reflects a king's unique status.[38]

---

33. In fact, the adage *Lechat'chilah ariber* was first used by the Rebbe Maharash in connection with commercial enterprise.
34. *Rambam, Mishneh Torah, Hilchos Melachim* 1:7.
35. *Ibid.* 11:1.
36. *Bamidbar* 24:17-18. See the essay entitled "The Function of *Mashiach*" in *I Await His Coming Every Day* (Kehot, N.Y., 1991) which develops the parallel between *Mashiach* and King David.
37. Cf. *Sefer HaSichos 5696,* p. 113.
38. See *Mishneh Torah, loc. cit.* 2:1. As in *Esther* 6:8-10, the crown is the most distinctive symbol of kingship. See the *maamar* entitled *Yaviu Levush Malchus,* ch. 23, in *Shaarei Orah, Shaar Purim.*

The Rebbe Rashab also shares a connection with *Mashiach,* as is highlighted by his conception of the students of Yeshivas Tomchei Temimim, the *yeshivah* he established in Lubavitch in 1897, as "soldiers of the House of David" whose primary goal is to bring about the coming of *Mashiach.*[39]

Shemini Atzeres: King Shlomo and the Rebbe Rayatz

The leaders associated with Shemini Atzeres, King Shlomo and the Previous Rebbe,[40] follow the *Ushpizin* of the previous day, for they continued and enhanced the contributions made by their respective fathers, King David and the Rebbe Rashab.

Though King David established the hereditary monarchy, his own reign was torn by strife and war; in the words of the prophet,[41] "You have shed blood." As to the reign of his son and successor King Shlomo, however, G-d promised,[42] "I will grant peace and tranquillity to Israel during his days." And indeed, throughout his reign,[43] "Israel dwelled in safety, every man under his vine and under his fig tree."

In this atmosphere of peace, King Shlomo built the *Beis HaMikdash,* a permanent dwelling place for G-d within our material world. This enabled the entire world to be refined, since the light generated by the *Beis HaMikdash* motivated people throughout the world to seek holiness.

In a similar way, the Previous Rebbe enhanced the achievements of his father, spreading the teachings of *Chas-*

---

39. See the renowned discourse entitled *Kol HaYotzei LeMilchemes Beis David* in *Sefer HaSichos 5702,* p. 141ff. [Appears in English translation in *With Light and with Might* (Kehot, N.Y., 1993)].
40. They are not referred to as *Ushpizin,* for that term (meaning "honored guests," and implying temporary influence only) is hardly appropriate for King Shlomo and the Previous Rebbe.
41. *I Divrei HaYamim* 28:4.
42. *Op. cit.* 22:9.
43. *I Melachim* 5:5.

sidus throughout the world, thereby preparing the world for the coming of the Redemption. No place was too far removed, nor any individual too estranged for the Rebbe Rayatz to reach out to him, and connect him with the teachings that herald and prepare us for the coming of *Mashiach.*

This is the legacy left to our present generation, and the goal to which all our efforts must be directed: to make the coming of the Redemption a tangible reality.[44] The coming of that era is not a matter of the distant future, but a present concern. For the time for the Redemption has arrived.[45]

May this promise be realized in the immediate future and may we then join in celebration with all the *Ushpizin* in *Eretz Yisrael,* in Jerusalem, and in the *Beis HaMikdash.*

---

44. See *Basi LeGani 5711* (in English translation; Kehot, N.Y., 1990).
45. Cf. *Yalkut Shimoni,* Vol. II, sec. 499, interpreting *Yeshayahu* 60:1.

Simchas Torah

JOY THAT KNOWS NO BOUNDS

Adapted from *Likkutei Sichos,*
Vol. IV,
Simchas Torah

Why does the Torah Remain Closed?

All reserve disappears in the exuberant dancing of Simchas Torah. Every Jew feels a natural desire to take a Torah scroll in his arms and celebrate. Hidden resources of joy, energies which we did not know we possessed, surface at this time.

The source for this happiness, the center of attention, is of course the Torah. Yet, throughout the entire *Hakkafos* celebrations, the Torah is never opened; we dance holding it wrapped in its mantle. Furthermore, on Simchas Torah people do not usually add to their usual schedule of Torah study; if anything, the opposite is true. Though the Torah is usually associated with disciplined study, on Simchas Torah we approach it differently, singing and dancing in a manner that bears no apparent relationship to understanding.[1]

The Core of the Torah

The reason for these innovations on Simchas Torah is that intellect is not the only means through which a person can connect with the Torah. One dimension of the Torah can be defined and grasped by our minds; another dimension is infinite, beyond all human comprehension. The infinite

---

1.   See *Sefer HaMaamarim 5686*, p. 55.

aspect of the Torah represents its essence, for "G-d and His Torah are one."[2]

Just as G-d is infinite, transcending all bounds and limitations, so too is the Torah, extending beyond the confines of human understanding. Accordingly, for man to relate to Torah, his commitment must mirror this infinity. Thus, when our ancestors received the Torah at Mt. Sinai they declared,[3] *Naaseh venishma* ("We will do and we will listen"), thereby making a superrational commitment to follow G-d's will, a commitment that was not conditional upon their understanding. By first stating *Naaseh* ("We will do"), they demonstrated that they were willing to follow G-d's commands without reservation.

The intellectual dimension of the Torah is crucial, but does not define its essence. So that man could relate to G-dliness, the Torah was brought down from its infinite heights and invested in rational concepts, laws and principles that can be studied, understood and incorporated into our behavior. These, however, represent merely the external dimensions of Torah and not its inner core.[4]

Garbing the Torah in intellectual categories is a process of outreach by G-d to man. On Simchas Torah, however, man reaches out to G-d and attempts to connect with the aspect of Torah that is one with Him. This requires stepping beyond the restrictions of one's own rational mindset. And this is precisely what takes place when a Jew dances with a Torah scroll on Simchas Torah.[5]

---

2. *Zohar* I, 24a; II, p. 60a; see also *Tanya*, chs. 4 and 23.
3. *Shmos* 24:7; *Shabbos* 88a.
4. From this perspective, there is no difference between a verse a child learns from the *Chumash* and a Talmudic dissertation delivered by a sage. Both are media in which G-d has invested Himself to allow man to relate to Him. The core of both experiences is not the simplicity or sophistication of the medium, but the inner bond with G-d that is established.
5. Afterwards, however, the Torah must be studied closely so that this essential bond is integrated into one's thought processes. Indeed, the *Hakkafos* circle the dais on which the Torah is read and they are introduced by a responsive reading of the

Dancing Together as One

All Jews, learned and unsophisticated alike, share equally in the Simchas Torah celebrations, because these celebrations tap a point in the soul which, by nature of its infinity, defies the entire concept of rank and gradation. At this level of soul, no difference exists between one Jew and another. The basic commonalty that links us all makes us join hands and dance together, oblivious to the personal differences that might otherwise create barriers between individuals.[6]

The "Feet" of the Torah

The Previous Rebbe used to say[7] that on Simchas Torah, the Torah itself wants to dance; however, since a Torah scroll has no feet, we Jews must function as its feet and carry it around the dais in the synagogue.[8]

A foot has no independent will; it is totally subservient to the head that controls it, obeying its wishes without question. So deep and complete is our surrender to the Torah on Simchas Torah, that we are lifted beyond the realm of our individual identities and become the "feet of the Torah."

This metaphor reminds one of the need to advance in Torah throughout the entire year, for the feet are associated with marching forward. This progress affects the Torah as well as the Jewish people, for just as the feet can bring the head to a place it cannot reach alone, the Jewish people can elevate the Torah and bring its essence to the surface.

---

verses beginning *Atah hareisa.* These practices are a reminder that even the boundless celebrations of Simchas Torah remain connected with the Torah's intellectual content; the rational and superrational dimensions of the Torah cannot be separated from each other.

6. See the above essay entitled "The Unity of our People," which speaks of the unique element of Jewish unity that characterizes Simchas Torah.

7. *Sefer HaSichos 5704,* p. 36.

8. Thus we can understand the description of the holiday as "the season of *our* rejoicing": not only is this happiness shared by the entire Jewish people, but the Torah itself also shares in this joy.

Landing Safely

In light of this, we can appreciate the place of Simchas Torah in the sequence of holidays beginning with Rosh HaShanah and Yom Kippur. All of these holidays focus our attention on the inner core of our relationship with G-d. Simchas Torah, as their climax, is the point of transition between the intense spiritual experience of the month of Tishrei and our daily, down-to-earth circumstances.

This safe landing is navigated by means of the rejoicing of Simchas Torah. At that time, our joyous awareness of how "Israel, the Torah, and the Holy One, blessed be He, are one,"[9] lays the groundwork for our divine service throughout the entire year. These celebrations enhance the bond with G-d and the Torah that is unconfined by the limits of intellect, in every aspect of our conduct throughout the year.

Moreover, these celebrations anticipate the ultimate celebrations that will accompany the coming of *Mashiach* and the advent of the Era of the Redemption. May this take place in the immediate future.

---

9.   Cf. *Zohar* III, 73a.

HAPPINESS WHICH WE HAVE EARNED

Adapted from *Likkutei Sichos,*
Vol. XIV,
Simchas Torah

Shavuos and Simchas Torah: Two Approaches

Shavuos and Simchas Torah are both devoted to deepening our appreciation of the Torah. The celebrations of these two holidays, however, differ dramatically. Shavuos is characterized by a sober increase in Torah study. In many communities it is customary to remain awake through the first night of Shavuos to study the Torah. In contrast, the celebration of Simchas Torah does not typically involve increased Torah study. It is, instead, marked by unbounded happiness, singing, and dancing.

These different customs echo a more fundamental difference in the divine service of these two holidays. Shavuos, as "the season of the Giving of our Torah,"[1] focuses on the Giver of the Torah. Simchas Torah, by contrast, celebrating the completion of the annual cycle of Torah readings, demonstrates how man can succeed in his Torah study through his own efforts. Thus it is appended to Sukkos, "the season of our rejoicing."

G-d's Torah, and Man's Striving to Possess It

The contrast between these two perspectives on our relationship with the Torah can be illustrated by examples from

---

1. The festival liturgy.

Torah law. Our Sages[2] state that a person who is ritually impure is permitted to study Torah since the Torah itself cannot be rendered impure. "My words (i.e., the Torah) are like fire,"[3] and "just as fire cannot become impure, likewise the words of Torah cannot contract impurity." The Torah remains G-d's word even when spoken by an impure individual; his impurity does not detract from the Torah's fundamental G-dly nature.

Conversely, our Sages[4] state that a Torah scholar is allowed to forego the honor due to him. One might suppose that since any token of respect should relate to his Torah knowledge and not to himself, he should not be allowed to forego it. In fact, however, this ruling of the Sages implies that his knowledge is considered his own to the point where he can choose either to accept or reject such honor.[5]

These two points of *halachah* reflect different perspectives. The first perceives the Torah as a mirror of G-d's utterly transcendent infinity. The second perspective focuses on Torah as internalized by man and points to the ways in which his thinking and conduct can be modified thereby.[6]

No Longer the "Bread of Shame"

The second approach is more closely related to joy. Our Sages state:[7] "A person prefers one *kav*[8] of his own over nine that belong to someone else." He foregoes the greater quan-

---

2. *Berachos* 22a.
3. *Yirmeyahu* 23:29.
4. *Kiddushin* 32a.
5. *Avodah Zarah* 19a states that when a Torah scholar has completed his study of a subject, the Torah concepts which he has grasped are considered "his own, and identified with his name."
6. This, after all, is the purpose of Torah study — to upgrade one's thought processes and ultimately, one's actual conduct; as our Sages declare (*Berachos* 17a): "The ultimate goal of wisdom is *teshuvah* and good deeds."
7. *Bava Metzia* 38a.
8. A Talmudic measure.

tity because of the fulfillment he feels when he receives something that he has worked for and earned.

From the perspective of G-d, the Giver of the Torah, the Torah completely bypasses the confines of man's limited understanding. However, when a person relates to the Torah from this perspective, he experiences it as the "bread of shame"[9] — alms received as charity, a gift that he has not earned. If, instead, he works hard at studying Torah so that he can thoroughly grasp it, the satisfaction he feels corresponds directly to the effort he has expended.

This is why Simchas Torah is celebrated with such joy. Our efforts to comprehend the Torah throughout the entire year are now consummated — surely a cause for unlimited rejoicing.

The Distinctive Quality of the Second Tablets

The above-described differences between Shavuos and Simchas Torah also relate to another explanation for the celebration of Simchas Torah,[10] namely, that it commemorates the giving of the second tablets on Yom Kippur.[11]

Extolling the first tablets, our Sages state[12] that had they not been broken, "The Torah would never have been forgotten by the Jewish people...and no other nation would ever have ruled over them."

The second tablets are significant for a different reason. Our Sages explain[13] that with the first tablets only the Five Books of Moshe and the Book of Yehoshua were revealed. The revelation of the second tablets, however, comprised the

---

9.   Cf. *Jerusalem Talmud, Orlah* 1:3.

10. See *Or HaTorah* on Shemini Atzeres, p. 1779; *Sefer HaMaamarim 5689*, p. 56ff.

11. See *Rashi* on *Taanis* 26b. The celebration is, however, delayed from Yom Kippur until Simchas Torah in order to allow the powerful spiritual influences aroused on Yom Kippur to be integrated within the Jewish people.

12. *Eruvin* 54a.

13. *Nedarim* 22b.

entire Oral Law, the realm of Torah that allows for man's creative input. With the giving of the second tablets, therefore, fruitful effort in Torah study became necessary and possible.[14]

Accepting the Torah with Teshuvah

The first tablets were given to the Jewish people when, in the words of our Sages,[15] "Their impurity had ceased," and they were on the level of *tzaddikim,* "righteous men." The second tablets, by contrast, were given after they had committed the sin of the Golden Calf and repented. At this point their divine service followed the path of *baalei teshuvah,* those who turn to G-d in repentance.

Unlike the *tzaddik,* the *baal teshuvah* must rely primarily on his own efforts. The divine service of the *tzaddik* is aided by the natural tendency within man to act righteously. Since this tendency is weakened through sin, the *baal teshuvah* has to summon up inner energies in his striving to develop a new bond with G-d.

Beginning Creation Anew

Immediately after completing the year-long Reading of the Torah we start again:[16] "In the beginning, G-d created the heavens and the earth." This reading reminds us of man's input in Torah, for it is through our efforts in the study and practice of Torah that we become G-d's partners in creation,[17] transforming the world into a dwelling place for Him.[18]

---

14. Further to the concept of human achievement: *Rashi* comments on *Shmos* 34:1 that whereas the first tablets were "the work of G-d," the second tablets were hewn out by Moshe.
15. *Shabbos* 146a.
16. *Bereishis* 1:1.
17. See *Shabbos* 11a, 119b; see also *Likkutei Sichos,* Vol. XV, p. 95.
18. Cf. *Midrash Tanchuma, Parshas Bechukosai,* sec. 3; *Tanya,* chs. 33 and 36.

The ultimate expression of the world as G-d's dwelling place will come in the Era of the Redemption, when we will merit the revelation of "the new heaven and the new earth which I (G-d) will make."[19] May this take place in the immediate future.

---

19. *Yeshayahu* 66:22.

Yud-Tes Kislev

BRIDGING THE GAP BETWEEN THE
INTELLECT AND SELF-TRANSCENDENCE

Adapted from *Likkutei Sichos,*
Vol. IV, *Chai* Elul;
Kuntreis Inyanah shel Toras HaChassidus

A Sign of Divine Approval

Yud-Tes Kislev commemorates the nullification of the capital sentence against the Alter Rebbe, founder of the *Chabad*-Lubavitch chassidic movement, and his liberation from imprisonment in the year 5559 (1798). The Alter Rebbe had been arrested by the czarist authorities for spreading Chassidism throughout Russia, creating a movement which they perceived as threatening the Czar's authority.

Like every event in the temporal world, the Alter Rebbe's arrest was a reflection of events taking place in the spiritual realm. While in prison the Alter Rebbe was visited by the souls of his predecessors, the Baal Shem Tov, founder of Chassidism, and his successor, the Maggid of Mezritch.[1] When he asked them why he had been arrested, they explained that his manner of teaching chassidic thought had aroused a *kitrug;* i.e., its legitimacy had been challenged in the Heavenly Court.

Before his imprisonment the Alter Rebbe had been teaching Torah's mystical secrets openly to the masses, and the objection had been raised that the world was not suffi-

---

1. See *Beis Rebbe,* Vol. I, ch. 16, note 2; see also the explanation of this concept in *Likkutei Sichos,* Vol. XXX, p. 170ff.

ciently refined to receive these spiritual truths. This *kitrug* had resulted in the Alter Rebbe's arrest.

When the Alter Rebbe heard this explanation, he asked whether or not he should continue his teaching upon his release. The Baal Shem Tov explained that if the Alter Rebbe were duly released this would be a sign of Divine acceptance of his actions and that he should continue "with greater intensity and power." Shortly afterwards, the Russian government dropped the charges against the Alter Rebbe and he was released on *Yud-Tes* Kislev. Since then, this date has been commemorated as a major chassidic holiday, a day from which to draw inspiration.[2]

A Point of Transition

Yud-Tes Kislev marked a turning point in the Alter Rebbe's approach to teaching. After his release, he began to deliver longer discourses and to present chassidic thought within an intellectual framework, rather than as brief articles of faith. The Rebbe Rashab, the fifth Lubavitcher Rebbe, held that the fundamental service of "spreading the wellsprings of *Chassidus* outward" began after the Alter Rebbe's release on *Yud-Tes* Kislev.[3]

On one occasion,[4] the Rebbe Rashab stated that before *Yud-Tes* Kislev, "*Chassidus* used to scorch the world": its transcendent, spiritual nature could not be contained within the thought patterns prevalent in the material world, and in fact, contradicted them. From *Yud-Tes* Kislev onward, however, the Alter Rebbe garbed his teachings in a form that could be

---

2. The Previous Rebbe quotes the Alter Rebbe as saying that *Yud-Tes* Kislev "will be established as a festival of continuing [relevance] among the Jewish people." It is a day when "thousands of Jewish hearts will be aroused to *teshuvah* and heartfelt divine service" (*Likkutei Dibburim*; English translation (Kehot, N.Y., 1987), Vol. I, p. 45).
3. *Toras Shalom*, p. 112.
4. *Ibid.*, p. 26.

grasped intellectually, enabling anyone, even a spiritually insensitive person, to approach and comprehend the Torah's deepest mystical secrets.

The Alter Rebbe named his approach *Chabad,* an acronym for the Hebrew words "wisdom, understanding, and knowledge," thereby highlighting the intellect as a medium for connecting with G-d.

An Extension or a Departure?

At first glance, the Alter Rebbe's approach appears to depart from the main thrust of the Baal Shem Tov's teachings. The Baal Shem Tov taught that[5] "G-d desires the heart."[6] He extolled the simple faith and unreserved commitment of the common man, and explained that these could establish a deeper and more powerful bond with G-d than a scholar's endeavors. The Alter Rebbe's emphasis on the importance of the mind appears to be a change of course, a retreat from the vitality of the heart to the reserve of the intellect.

The Alter Rebbe himself saw no contradiction between his teachings and those of the Baal Shem Tov. On the contrary, he would refer to himself as the Baal Shem Tov's grandson.[7] When challenged by R. Baruch of Mezhibuzh, the Baal Shem Tov's biological grandson, the Alter Rebbe replied, "You may be his grandson in a physical sense; I am his grandson in a spiritual sense."

The Alter Rebbe's perception of himself as the spiritual heir of the Baal Shem Tov sheds light on the connection between *Chabad* Chassidism and the Baal Shem Tov. While the essence of parents is manifested in their children, children do more than passively receive. They contribute to the legacy received from their parents, enhancing it with their

5. *Sefer HaMaamarim 5711,* p. 311.
6. Cf. *Sanhedrin* 106b; *Zohar* II, 182b.
7. See *HaTamim,* Vol. II, p. 56.

own powers. The Alter Rebbe received the essence of the Baal Shem Tov's teachings but also contributed to them, extending their scope to include the realm of intellect as well as the realm of the heart.

An Expression of the Soul's Infinity

Given the apparent contradiction between head and heart, how can the spiritual emotions encouraged by the Baal Shem Tov be reconciled with the intellectual approach of *Chabad?*

This question can be answered by an analysis of the potentials we possess within our souls. Certain of our potentials, such as our intellects and emotions, are defined and limited. The soul's essence, however, stands above these and all other limits, for the soul is "an actual part of G-d," and just as G-d cannot be defined or limited in any way, neither can our souls.

Accordingly, the soul cannot be reduced to being defined or identified with any particular human quality. By the same token, however, this potential cannot be defined as completely transcending all our other potentials since this, too, would constitute a limitation of the soul's powers. The soul must be capable of pervading the entire realm of conscious human potential, revealing its unlimited power within this limited context. Otherwise, the existence of this limited framework would appear to be a barrier to the boundless essence of the soul.[8]

On this basis, we can understand the transition from the teachings of the Baal Shem Tov to the philosophy of *Chabad* Chassidism. The Baal Shem Tov stirred the essence of the Jewish soul, revealing a realm of experience beyond the range

---

8. Similarly, speaking of the essence of G-d's infinite light, the *Avodas HaKodesh* (Vol. I, ch. 8) states: "The *Or Ein Sof* is the quintessence of all perfection. Just as it has an infinite dimension, it has a finite dimension. For were one to presume that it has an infinite dimension, but no finite dimension, one would detract from its perfection."

of our conscious powers. Once revealed, however, this transcendent essence of the soul needs to be internalized and integrated within our conscious powers as well — and this process begins with our intellectual faculties. This was accomplished through the Alter Rebbe's teachings, especially through the new approach to his teachings that followed his release on *Yud-Tes* Kislev.

Above, But Not Beyond

However, the focus of *Chabad* on intellectual endeavor does not limit *Chassidus* to the constraints of human thought. Instead, it shows how the study and practice of *Chassidus* can transform the nature of our thoughts and expand our intellectual potential to the point where it can relate to essential G-dliness.

Intellect allows people to grow and communicate. By developing an intellectual framework for chassidic thought, the Alter Rebbe made it possible for the Baal Shem Tov's teachings to permeate the full scope of our personalities and to be shared with other people.

In light of this, we can understand the choice of oil as a metaphor for *Chassidus*. Oil has two distinctive qualities: it does not mix with any other liquid and it can penetrate all matter. The same is true of the teachings of *Chabad* Chassidism. It reveals the essence of our souls, the highest of our potentials. The Alter Rebbe's contribution enables this potential to influence and affect the functioning of all our powers, and thus be expressed in every aspect of our lives.

Precipitating the Redemption

With this in mind, we can understand why the coming of the Redemption is related to the revelation and spreading of

Chassidism.[9] In the Era of the Redemption, G-d's purpose in the creation of the world will be revealed.[10] And why did G-d create the world? — Because He "desired a dwelling in the lower worlds."[11]

It is at home that a person reveals his true self. Hence, in describing G-d's desire for a dwelling as the purpose for creation, our Sages implied that He desires that His essence be revealed.[12] Furthermore, He desires that this revelation take place "in the lower worlds," i.e., in our physical world. Hence, it is important that this revelation be perceived and understood by man, a critical element of this lower realm.

In the Era of the Redemption, both of these desires will be realized: G-d's essence will be revealed and that revelation will pervade the entire creation. In order to hasten those revelations, we must manifest similar qualities in our present divine service, for the Torah's rewards are granted "measure for measure."[13]

On the human level, this means making use of the Baal Shem Tov's revelation of the essence of the soul, and making use of the Alter Rebbe's revelation of our ability to internalize this essence by intellectual effort. Through these teachings, we and our environment can become a "dwelling for G-d," and prepare for the extension of that dwelling throughout the world with the coming of *Mashiach*. May this take place in the immediate future.

---

9.   See the letter of the Baal Shem Tov to his brother-in-law, R. Gershon Kitover (reproduced in part in *Keser Shem Tov*, sec. 1), which teaches that the coming of *Mashiach* depends on the dissemination of the wellsprings of Chassidism to the outermost limits.

10. *Tanya*, ch. 36.

11. *Midrash Tanchuma, Parshas Bechukosai*, sec. 3, cited in *Tanya, loc. cit.*

12. *Sefer Mamaarim 5565*, Vol. I, p. 489, and other sources.

13. *Sanhedrin* 90a.

"HE HAS REDEEMED MY SOUL IN PEACE"

Adapted from *Likkutei Sichos,*
Vol. XV,
Parshas Vayishlach

Far from Coincidence

In a letter[1] to R. Levi Yitzchak of Berditchev, written after his release from prison on *Yud-Tes* Kislev, the Alter Rebbe described the moment at which he was informed of his release by the czarist authorities as follows: "As I was reciting *Tehillim,* reading the verse that begins,[2] 'He has redeemed my soul in peace,' and before I began the following verse, I went forth in peace through the G-d of Peace."

The connection between *Yud-Tes* Kislev and peace explains an important effect of the new approach to teaching *Chassidus* that was introduced on that date. Before *Yud-Tes* Kislev, fragmentation was rampant in many areas of Jewish life; the teachings of Chassidism, as we shall see, bridged gaps on all sides.

Oneness in the Torah

The study of the Torah is broadly divided into two disciplines: *nigleh* ("the revealed dimension" — Torah law) and *pnimiyus haTorah* ("the inner dimension of Torah" — the mysticism of the Kabbalah.)

---

1. *Igros Kodesh* (Letters) of the Alter Rebbe, p. 98.
2. 55:19.

Before the rise of Chassidism, the study of *pnimiyus haTorah* was not as widespread as that of the *Talmud*. Scholars whose entire lives were devoted to the study of the *Talmud* and its commentaries may never have been exposed to the mystical teachings of the Kabbalah. Even a sage who studied both areas and whose appreciation of Torah law was influenced by his study of *pnimiyus haTorah,* considered the two to be separate disciplines. The teachings of the Alter Rebbe integrated both realms of study, joining "the body of Torah" *(nigleh)* with its "soul" *(pnimiyus haTorah)* to form one cohesive organism.[3]

Oneness in Our People

A similar pattern can be seen in Jewish communal life: the revelation of chassidic teachings brought our people closer to each other, erasing previous differences. Before the rise of Chassidism, the common people, the *amcha Yidden* who were the broad and solid base of every Jewish community, felt estranged from the scholars and Torah leaders. Though scholars taught them Torah and no doubt taught proper conduct by example, scholars maintained their distance, closeted away with their learned books, uninvolved in the affairs of the common people.

Chassidism brought these two groups together. Scholars began to show concern for the material, as well as the spiritual, welfare of the common man.[4] And they began to gear their teachings to the level of those less learned, clothing the

---

3. Cf. *Zohar* III, 152a, regarding the expressions "the soul of the Torah" and "the body of the Torah."
4. Thus, before founding the chassidic movement, the Baal Shem Tov headed a group of *nistarim,* scholars whose anonymous efforts on behalf of the common people included the provision of employment for them (*HaTamim,* Issue 2, p. 44). Similarly, after his marriage, the Alter Rebbe organized agricultural communities which enabled Jews to become self-sufficient (*Igros Kodesh* (Letters) of the Rebbe Rayatz, Vol. VI, p. 418).

ideas of Torah — even the mysticism of *pnimiyus haTorah* —
in language that ordinary people could relate to.

Oneness in Our Souls

The impulse toward unity initiated by chassidic thought
also affects our personal divine service. The service of G-d
finds expression through two seemingly separate channels,
intellect and faith. At one level, our conduct is governed by
our minds; faith connects us to G-d through an expression of
the soul that transcends the limits of our minds.

Chassidic thought enables us to see that these two channels are not contradictory, and shows us how to integrate the
two so that we can develop ourselves fully. The transcendent
quality of faith can also permeate the realm of intellect,
thereby enabling even the mind to apprehend the spiritual.

An Expression of the Essence

The unity with which Chassidism was able to suffuse
Judaism and Jewish communal life results from its emphasis
on the *essential core* of the Torah and of the soul. Only a
superficial perspective can perceive *nigleh* and *pnimiyus haTorah* as separate disciplines. Focusing on the essence of Torah
enables us to appreciate how its revealed and mystical planes
enhance each other, making a complete bond with Torah
possible.[5]

Likewise in the area of Jewish oneness: Differences
between people are perceived only when one looks at their
intellectual and emotional characteristics, for at that level, no
two people are alike. At the level of the essence of souls,
however, we are all joined in a fundamental unity. Both

---

5. "It must be apparent that an individual studying *nigleh* has studied *Chassidus.*
   Likewise, it must be apparent that a person studying *Chassidus* has studied *nigleh*"
   (*Igros Kodesh* (Letters) of the Rebbe Rayatz, Vol. X, pp. 4, 366, 368).

scholar and common man possess the same fundamental G-dly spark.

And likewise with regard to every individual: Focusing on the essence of the soul enables us to perceive the human personality as a unified whole, in which faith and intellect complement each other to enable the individual to develop an all-encompassing bond with G-d.

"Spreading the Wellsprings Outward"

The above emphasis of chassidic thought on the essence of the Torah and the essence of the soul makes it possible to "spread the wellsprings of Chassidism outward." In its broadest sense, this means extending the teachings of Chassidism to individuals who are estranged from their Jewish heritage.

Chassidus enables even a person with a limited understanding of Torah to appreciate the Torah's deepest truths because *Chassidus* relates to the essence of the soul, a potential which remains active in every individual no matter how he conducts himself in his daily life. Regardless of his level of observance, every Jew shares an essential connection with G-d.[6] Chassidic thought can nurture this essential connection and bring it into expression in one's daily life.

The Era of Redemption will witness the ultimate expression of the essential bond our world shares with G-d. By "spreading the wellsprings outward," revealing this essential connection within the Torah and the Jewish people, we can anticipate this era and hasten its coming. May this take place in the immediate future.

---

6.   *Sanhedrin* 44a.

Chanukah

THE MESSAGE OF THE CHANUKAH LIGHTS

Adapted from *Likkutei Sichos,*
Vol. I, Chanukah;
Likkutei Sichos, Vol. V, Chanukah;
the *Sichos* of *Shabbos* Chanukah, 5739

"A Mitzvah is a Lamp"

On Chanukah, the Previous Rebbe would tell his chassidim,[1] "We must listen carefully to what the candles are saying." In fact, the message of the Chanukah lights affects the entire scope of our service of G-d throughout the year, for "a *mitzvah* is a lamp and Torah is light."[2] Though every *mitzvah* is a lamp which lights up the darkness of our material world, this illumination is more manifest in those *mitzvos* which are associated with visible light.

The spiritual implications of the Chanukah lights are reflected in the halachic details that regulate the performance of the *mitzvah*. For a start, the Chanukah lights should be kindled after sunset and must burn into the night.[3] Furthermore, they should be placed "at the outside of the entrance to one's home,"[4] which shows that they are primarily intended to illuminate the public domain rather than one's own home.

The darkness of night and the public domain represent the aspects of our material existence which obscure G-dly light and prevent us from appreciating G-d's all-pervasive unity. By kindling Chanukah candles, we generate light

---

1. *Kuntreis Baruch SheAsah Nissim* (Kehot, N.Y., 5711).
2. *Mishlei* 6:23.
3. See *Shabbos* 21b; *Shulchan Aruch, Orach Chayim* 672:1-2.
4. *Shabbos, loc. cit.*

which elevates the material realm and reveals its G-dly nature.

No other *mitzvah* so directly elevates those aspects of material existence which conceal G-dliness. The positive commandments of the Torah affect only things which are by nature fit to be elevated. For this reason, positive command- ments cannot be fulfilled with materials that are not kosher.[5] Even the Torah's prohibitions, the commandments that are concerned with material elements which cannot be refined, do not elevate these negative forces; the purpose of these prohibitions is merely to negate their influence. The Chanu- kah candles, however, are able to refine and elevate the dark- ness of the public domain, causing it to shine with G-dly light.

To Make the Darkness Glow

The unique power of the Chanukah lights is linked to the nature of the miracle they commemorate. The miracle of Chanukah took place in a time of darkness, when the Greeks, who had conquered the Land of Israel, sought to impose their culture upon its inhabitants. Despite the assimilatory influ- ence of Jewish Hellenists, the Maccabees were able to instill in the Jewish people a spirit of *mesirus nefesh* (self-sacrifice) and *teshuvah* (return to G-d). This inspired them to fight the Greeks, defeat them, and rededicate the *Beis HaMikdash*. Since the Jewish victory involved the transformation of dark- ness into light, the Chanukah lights which commemorate it also have this power.

And they teach us that when confronted with darkness, we must not resign ourselves to it. Nor may we remain con- tent with lighting up our own homes. Instead, we must reach out and spread light as far as we possibly can, until the public domain too is illuminated.

---

5.   *Shabbos* 28b.

Transcending Even Spiritual Self-Interest

The Chanukah hymn beginning *HaNeiros Hallalu*[6] records
another halachic requirement: "These lights are holy and we
are not permitted to make use of them, only to look at them."
I.e., though the Chanukah candles must burn into the night,
when their light would be useful, we are not allowed to make
use of it. To ensure this, we light an extra candle, the *shamash,* and place it above the others, so that any unintentional
benefit from the light is attributable to the *shamash*[7] and not
the lamps lit for the performance of the *mitzvah.*

These laws reflect the unique nature of this *mitzvah.*
Though every *mitzvah* earns a reward, in certain cases the
reward is spiritual, while in others it is also manifest in the
material world. The visible light of the Chanukah candles
indicates that the positive effects generated by this *mitzvah*
are apparent in our material world as well as in the spiritual
realm.

However, just as we do not make use of the light of the
Chanukah lights for mundane purposes, our goal in performing this *mitzvah* is not material reward. We fulfill it only
because "You have sanctified us with Your commandments
and commanded us,"[8] without thought of reward or any other
ulterior motive. This level of performance, *avodah lishmah*
("divine service for its own sake"), is the highest that can be
attained through our own spiritual endeavors.[9]

Like much human behavior, even our divine service may
be motivated by a desire for spiritual, if not material, rewards.
The Chanukah lights teach us to transcend our tendencies
toward self-interest and dedicate ourselves to serving G-d for
His sake alone. The Chanukah lights, which burn in the
darkness of the night, demonstrate moreover that we can

6. *Siddur Tehillat HaShem,* p. 339.
7. *Shulchan Aruch, Orach Chayim* 673:1.
8. The wording of the blessing recited before the performance of a *mitzvah.*
9. *Rambam, Mishneh Torah, Hilchos Teshuvah* 10:4-5.

reach this advanced level of divine service, not only during daylight (which symbolizes manifest G-dliness), but also in times when effort is necessary to transform the darkness around us.

Attaining the Heights of Divine Service

Another halachic consideration: The custom in all Jewish homes is to add one candle every night to the number of candles lit the previous night. This custom is universal, even though technically, the minimum halachic requirement may be satisfied by lighting only one candle on each of the nights of Chanukah.[10] Our practice thus follows the style of the *mehadrin* ("those who are lovingly punctilious") and who embellish the *mitzvah* by sparing neither expense nor effort in observing it.

There is, moreover, a higher level of fulfilling the *mitzvah,* the manner of those who are *mehadrin min hamehadrin* ("the most punctilious of all"), who display a level of *hiddur* which surpasses the above-mentioned level of the *mehadrin.*

Performing the *mitzvah* on the superior level of *mehadrin min hamehadrin* involves adding a new candle every night for each member of the household.[11] Significantly, it is common practice today for everyone to kindle the Chanukah lights in this fashion.[12] Throughout the Jewish world, even in circles where the observance of many other *mitzvos* leaves room for improvement, this *mitzvah* is commonly observed on the level of *mehadrin min hamehadrin.*

Our ability to fulfill this *mitzvah* in this manner was bequeathed to us by the Maccabees. When they rededicated the *Beis HaMikdash,* Torah law would have permitted them to

---

10. *Shabbos* 21b; *Rambam, Mishneh Torah, Hilchos Chanukah* 4:1; *Tur Shulchan Aruch, Orach Chayim* 671:2..

11. *Op. cit.*

12. *Rama, Orach Chayim* 671:2.

light the golden *Menorah* with ritually impure oil. For the obligation to kindle the *Menorah* in a state of ritual purity is, as we also find with regard to the communal offerings, waived when there is no alternative.[13] The Maccabees, however, refused to be satisfied with the minimum fulfillment of the *mitzvah*. Determined to kindle the *Menorah* as perfectly as possible, as befits *mehadrin min hamehadrin*, they decided to use only pure oil.

To make this possible, since preparing fresh oil took eight days, G-d intervened in the natural order and performed the Chanukah miracle: a single cruse with enough pure olive oil to last one day remained burning for eight days. We commemorate this miracle by following the Maccabees' example and kindling our Chanukah lights in the manner of *mehadrin min hamehadrin*.

To Continually Increase Light

Adding a new Chanukah candle every night teaches us that every day we must increase our endeavors to spread light throughout the world. Though we lit up our environment on the previous night, even at the level of *mehadrin min hamehadrin*, we cannot rest content. As our Sages explain,[14] lighting the Chanukah candles exemplifies the principle, "Always advance higher in holy matters."

Beginning with the second night of Chanukah (the first time we add a candle), we express this principle for an entire week, increasing the number of candles every night. A week is a complete time cycle[15] which contains in potential form all the possible situations a person might encounter. Adding a new light on every night of Chanukah demonstrates — and

13. *Zevachim* 22b; *Rambam, Hilchos Bias HaMikdash* 4:9.
14. *Shabbos, loc. cit.*
15. See *Sefer HaMaamarim 5678*, p. 269ff.; *5704*, p. 192 ff.

reinforces — a commitment to progress continuously, come what may.

The lessons we learn from the Chanukah lights should be applied in every aspect of our lives. Every day should lead us to further growth and create new opportunities for spreading G-dly light in our homes and in the world. Thus understood, the kindling of the Chanukah lights will serve as a catalyst to bring about the ultimate light that will illuminate the world in the Era of the Redemption.

Chanukah is bound to the Era of Redemption by the number eight, which is both the number of nights on which we light Chanukah candles and a number intimately associated with that ultimate age.[16] Our kindling of Chanukah candles both anticipates and precipitates the Era when "a priest will appear in Zion"[17] and light the *Menorah* in the *Beis HaMikdash*. May this take place in the immediate future.

---

16. *Arachin* 13b; *Or HaTorah* on Chanukah, 326b ff.
17. A traditional blessing used throughout the ages.

WHY THE MACCABEES REBELLED:
A SUPERRATIONAL COMMITMENT
TO THE TORAH

Adapted from *Likkutei Sichos,*
Vol. III, Chanukah;
Vol. X, p. 291;
the *maamar* entitled *LeHavin Inyan Chanukah 5739;*
Letters of the Lubavitcher Rebbe *Shlita* (in English), pp. 204-207

Why did the Greeks Defile the Oil?

Our Sages[1] describe the miracle of Chanukah as follows: During their occupation of the Holy Land, the Greeks entered the *Heichal* (the Sanctuary in the *Beis HaMikdash*) and defiled all the vessels of olive oil they found. After their defeat, the Maccabees were able to find only one cruse of oil with the seal of the High Priest intact. Though it contained enough oil for only one day, the rekindled *Menorah* burned miraculously for eight days, enough time for new oil to be prepared.

The *Talmud* clearly indicates that the Greeks' defiling of the oil was intentional and systematic; they neither used it nor destroyed it. What did they gain by defiling it?

A Spiritual Conflict

This question can be answered by analyzing the nature of the conflict between the Greeks and the Jews. While building their empire, the Greeks did not usually attempt to eradicate indigenous populations; their goal was to Hellenize and

---

1.   *Shabbos* 21b.

assimilate them into their culture. This was their policy when they imposed their rule over *Eretz Yisrael*.

This is why the prayer beginning *VeAl HaNissim*[2] states that the Greeks endeavored to force the Jews to "forget *Your Torah* and violate the decrees of *Your* will" — to forget the Torah as it is connected to G-d.

The Greeks appreciated the wisdom and beauty of the Torah. What they opposed was the concept of Torah as G-dly revelation. They would have liked the Jewish people to study Torah in the same way they would have studied human wisdom, insensitive to its G-dliness that transcends the bounds of intellect.

"The Decrees of Your Will"

Likewise, the Greeks did not object to the fulfillment of the commandments *per se,* recognizing that every culture, including their own, has rituals. Their antagonism was aroused by the idea that *mitzvos* are a unique means of connecting to G-d which take us beyond human limits.

This idea is alluded to in the phrase from *VeAl HaNissim* which speaks of *chukei retzonecha* ("the decrees of Your will"). There are three categories of commandments: *mishpatim* (lit., "judgments"), *eidos* (lit., "testimonials"), and *chukim* (lit., "decrees").[3] *Mishpatim* are the *mitzvos* which appeal to reason, such as the prohibitions against theft and murder. The *eidos* commemorate events in Jewish history, a means of reliving the past and grasping its significance; for example, eating *matzah* on Pesach. The *chukim* are those *mitzvos* which are superrational, "a decree from Me, [which] you have no permission to question."[4]

---

2. *Siddur Tehillat HaShem,* p. 59.
3. See *Ramban* on *Devarim* 6:20; *Sefer HaMaamarim 5701,* p. 51 ff.
4. *Rashi* on *Bamidbar* 19:2; cf. *Yoma* 67b, and *Tanchuma, Parshas Chukas,* sec. 7.

The *eidos* and the *mishpatim* enable us to relate to G-d through means we can rationally appreciate; the *chukim*, by contrast, require us to rise above the limitations of our understanding. And when we do so, these *mitzvos* connect us with G-d's infinite dimension. It was the observance of the *chukim* that irked the Greek mentality and countered their philosophy.[5]

Impure Light and the Battle Against It

In light of this, we can understand why the Greeks were so intent on defiling the oil. They wanted the *Menorah* to be lit with impure oil so that its light, symbolic of the light of Torah, would shine forth not in its pristine purity, but with a human, Greek touch.

The Jews responded to this challenge with *mesirus nefesh*, self-sacrifice that leaps beyond the limits of reason. Though they were pitted against the world's strongest military power, they were determined to fight, and even to surrender their lives, in order to be able to study "*Your* Torah" and carry out the "decrees of *Your* Will."

The Power of a Single Cruse of Oil

This power of *mesirus nefesh* is symbolized by the one cruse of oil which still bore the seal of the High Priest. In describing the obligations of the High Priest, the *Rambam* writes:[6] "His glory is to reside in the *Beis HaMikdash* through-

---

5.   Within the category of *chukim*, an approach existed that the Greeks could have accepted — observance based on the rationale that since the Torah is based on wisdom, the fulfillment of all of its *mitzvos* must be validly motivated. (This would include even those whose reasons defy our limited mortal perspective.)

   This rationale would not have run contrary to the Greek approach. The Jewish observance of *chukim*, is not, however, based on the existence of an underlying rationale, but rather, on a commitment to G-d that transcends the limits of understanding. Such an approach could not be accepted by the Greeks.

6.   *Rambam, Hilchos Klei HaMikdash* 5:7.

out the day, and to go home only at night.... His home must be in Jerusalem and he may not depart from [it]."

The name Yerushalayim (ירושלים) is a composite of the two Hebrew words *yirah* and *shalem* (יראה and שלם), together implying "complete awe."[7] The fact that the High Priest never leaves Jerusalem means that he never abandons this all-encompassing fear of G-d. Within each of our hearts, we all possess a similar quality. We, too, can relate to G-d with the intensity of the High Priest.

The potential to attain this level is our "one cruse of oil." It is hidden in every individual, begging to be discovered. Although a person might not uncover this internal connection to G-d in the ordinary circumstances of his life, when challenged, as in the case of the Maccabees, this inner connection will surface. And when this Divine bond comes to the fore, "[G-d will] deliver the mighty into the hands of the weak, the many into the hands of the few,"[8] for nothing can withstand its power.

In their struggle against the Greeks, the Maccabees tapped this resource — this single cruse of oil, revealing a level of soul that transcended their usual limits. In response, G-d revealed forces that transcended the natural limits of this world.

The Chanukah miracle which followed serves as an eternal testimony to the essential connection to G-d that the Greeks sought to sever. In our day as well, the Chanukah lights remind us that through "*Your* Torah" and "the decrees of *Your* will" — through an appreciation of the *infinite* dimension of the Torah and its commandments — we can develop a complete connection with G-d. Succeeding in this will lead us to the time when our bond with G-d will encompass all existence, for "the earth will be filled with the knowledge of G-d as the waters cover the ocean bed,"[9] with the

7. *Bereishis Rabbah, Parshas Bereishis,* sec. 56; *Tosafos* on *Taanis* 16a, s.v. *Har.*
8. The prayer beginning *VeAl HaNissim* (*Siddur Tehillat HaShem, loc. cit.*).
9. *Yeshayahu* 11:9.

coming of the Redemption. May this take place in the immediate future.

TWO MIRACLES:
TWO MODES OF COMMEMORATION

Adapted from *Likkutei Sichos,*
Vol. X, Chanukah;
Vol. XXV, Chanukah

The Chanukah Miracles

The *Rambam* describes the Chanukah miracle as follows:[1]

> 1. In [the era of] the Second *Beis HaMikdash,* the Greek kingdom issued decrees against the Jewish people, [attempting to] nullify their faith and refusing to allow them to observe the Torah and its commandments.

> [The Greeks] extended their hands against the property [of the Jews] and their daughters.... The Jews suffered great difficulties..., for [the Greeks] oppressed them severely until the G-d of our ancestors had mercy upon them, delivered them from [the] hands [of the Greeks] and saved them.

> The sons of the Hasmoneans, the High Priests, overcame [them], slew them, and saved the Jews from their hand....

> 2. When the Jews overcame their enemies and destroyed them, they entered the Sanctuary.... They could not find any pure oil in the Sanctuary, except for a single cruse. It contained enough oil to burn for only one day. They lit... the lamps with it for eight

---

1. *Rambam, Hilchos Megillah VeChanukah* 3:1.

days until they could crush olives and produce pure oil.

As may be seen from the wording of the *Rambam*, there are two miracles: the military victory in which G-d "delivered the mighty into the hands of the weak, and the many into the hands of the few,"[2] and the miracle through which the oil in the golden *Menorah* burned for eight days, rather than one.

Relating to the Material and the Spiritual

The *Rambam* concludes[3] that, in commemoration of these miracles, our Sages instituted the observance of the eight days of Chanukah as "days of happiness and praise [to G-d]," on which "lights should be kindled in the evening."

The commentaries on the *Rambam*[4] infer that "happiness and praise" represent two different modes of commemorating the miracles: "happiness" refers to the custom of holding celebratory feasts[5] during Chanukah, and "praise" refers to the recitation of the *Hallel.*[6] Since the military victory was material, it is celebrated physically, through eating and drinking; the miracle of the *Menorah* was spiritual and therefore, it is commemorated through spiritual activities — kindling lights and reciting the *Hallel.*[7]

---

2. The prayer beginning *VeAl HaNissim* (*Siddur Tehillat HaShem*, p. 59).

3. *Rambam, loc. cit.* 3:3.

4. *Yam Shel Shlomo* on *Bava Kama*, ch. 7, sec. 37; *Bayis Chadash, Orach Chayim,* sec. 670.

5. From the wording of the *Rambam* it appears that he maintains that it is a *mitzvah* to hold such feasts. The *Shulchan Aruch* (*Orach Chayim* 670:2, based on statements of Rabbeinu Asher and Rabbeinu Yitzchak Alfasi) differs, maintaining that no *mitzvah* is involved. The *Rama* cites other authorities who share the view of the *Rambam*, but for different reasons.

6. This is recited throughout all eight days of Chanukah (*Rambam, loc. cit.* 3:5; *Shulchan Aruch, loc. cit.* 683:1).

7. The recitation of *Hallel* also connects to the military victory as reflected in the prayer beginning *VeAl HaNissim*.

Light is the most spiritual element in our material world; though visible, it is not governed by the conventional laws of physical matter.[8] The spiritual aspect of the victory over the Greeks therefore found expression in the miracle of the lights of the *Menorah* of the *Beis HaMikdash,* and we commemorate this miracle by lighting Chanukah candles every year.

"What is Chanukah?"

The *Talmud*[9] emphasizes primarily the spiritual aspect of the Chanukah miracles. Our Sages ask: "What is Chanukah?" — I.e., for which miracle was the holiday instituted?[10] Their answer recounts the episode of the *Menorah* without elaborating on the military victory over the Greeks.

Although the miracle of the *Menorah* could not have taken place without the military victory, the victory itself does not define Chanukah. Chanukah is a holiday of spiritual light; even the war against the Greeks was essentially spiritual, since it was a struggle to preserve the Torah heritage from the taint of secular influence.[11]

This is why the prayer beginning *VeAl HaNissim,* which expresses thanks to G-d for the military victory, does not mention the spiritual miracle of the *Menorah,* for the latter eclipses it and is deserving of separate mention.[12] There is thus a separate means of commemoration for each of these two miracles.

---

8. This concept is reflected in the realm of *Halachah. Pesachim* 26a states that an image (which is transmitted through light rays) "has no substance."
9. *Shabbos* 21b.
10. *Rashi, loc. cit.*
11. See the above essay entitled, "Why the Maccabees Rebelled: A Superrational Commitment to the Torah."
12. According to this interpretation, the phrase (in *VeAl HaNissim*) "and they kindled lights in Your holy courtyards" does not refer to the lighting of the *Menorah* (for that was kindled in the Sanctuary building), but rather other lights kindled in celebration of the military victory. [The *Derashos* of the *Chasam Sofer* (p. 67a) offer a different interpretation.]

Body and Soul

The name Chanukah (חנוכה) shares the same root as the Hebrew word for "education" — *chinuch* (חינוך).[13] This implies a connection between the commemoration of this holiday and our ongoing personal growth, for Chanukah, like all the festivals, communicates a message that applies even after its celebration has concluded.

On a basic level, the message of Chanukah — that spiritual light can overpower military might — teaches us the supremacy of soul over body. Although we are a composite of body and soul and although the soul needs the medium of the body in order to express itself, the supremacy of the soul is not limited; the soul invigorates the body, and controls its functioning.[14]

By emphasizing only the miracle of the lights, our Sages highlight yet a deeper lesson. Chanukah grants every soul the potential to express itself without any hindrance from the material nature of the body. One can live and function in the world without being influenced by worldliness.[15] Chanukah enables us to live in the material world for the sake of a spiritual purpose, in the same way that the military victory over

---

13. The following essay develops this idea at length.
14. This concept has deeper significance pointing to — to borrow philosophic terms — the supremacy of form over matter. This principle lies at the heart of contemporary society, for in many areas, both in war and in peace, we have seen how superior thought, the medium with which we relate to form, can prevail over mere material power.

    This concept is paralleled in a halachic principle that *eichus* ("quality" or "inward virtue") is given precedence over *kamus* ("quantity").
15. Speaking of the halachic restrictions on transferring objects from one domain to another on *Shabbos,* our Sages (*Shabbos* 93b, as cited by *Rambam* in *Hilchos Shabbos* 18:28) state: "A person who transfers less than the standard measure [of a substance] is not liable even though he transfers it in a container. [Though he would have been liable had he transferred the container alone, here he is not liable, because] the container is subsidiary [to its contents]; [when the person transfers it,] he is concerned not with the container, but with what it contains."

    Similarly, concerning the connection between our bodies and our souls, we can regard our material activities as having no independent importance, and see them as nothing more than a medium for the expression of our divine service.

the Greeks was spiritually motivated. Chanukah further empowers us to make our lives within the world a medium for the expression of our spiritual service, like the miracle of the *Menorah*.

Living in this manner will hasten the coming of the era when this ability will spread throughout the world — in the Era of the Redemption, when "the earth will be filled with the knowledge of G-d as the waters cover the ocean bed."[16] May this take place in the immediate future.

---

16. *Yeshayahu* 11:9.

A New Level of Awareness

Adapted from the *Sichos* of
Chanukah, 5747

The Dedication of the Altar

In addition to the Maccabees' military victory over the
Greeks and the miracle of the *Menorah*, Chanukah commemorates the rededication of the *Beis HaMikdash*[1] and its
altar after it had been defiled by the Greeks.[2] Accordingly, the
name Chanukah (חנוכה) is derived from the word *chinuch*
(חנוך) which means not only "education" but also
"dedication". Dedication is also the theme of the passages
which the Sages chose for the daily reading of the Torah
during Chanukah.[3] They describe the inaugural offerings
brought by the tribal leaders of the Jewish people for the
dedication of the altar in the desert,[4] offerings which opened
up new spiritual possibilities for our material world.

---

1. *Shibalei HaLeket*, sec. 174; see also *Torah Or, Parshas Vayeishev* 29d.
2. *Darkei Moshe* and *Rama* (*Orach Chayim* 670:1); *Maharsha, Chiddushei Aggados*, on
    Sanhedrin 21b; *Torah Or, loc. cit.*
      According to the *Rama*, it is because of the dedication of the *Menorah* that Cha-
    nukah should be celebrated by festive gatherings and feasts.
3. *Bamidbar*, ch. 7.
4. See *Yalkut Shimoni, Melachim*, sec. 184, which states that the twenty-fifth of Kislev
    also marks the date of the completion of the Sanctuary erected in the desert.
    Although the Sanctuary was not erected until Nissan, G-d promised this day, the
    twenty-fifth of Kislev, that He would repay it at a later time. That debt was duly
    paid with the Maccabees' dedication of the altar on that date.

Why was the Chanukah Miracle Necessary?

The concept underlying the dedication of the altar helps us understand the Maccabean rededication of the *Beis HaMikdash.*

The kindling of the *Menorah* (like the offering of communal sacrifices) may be practiced in a state of ritual impurity when there is no other alternative.[5] Why, then, was the Chanukah miracle necessary?

Among the answers offered to this question[6] is that this leniency applies only to sacrifices brought upon an existing altar and to lights kindled upon an existing *Menorah.* However, when the *Beis HaMikdash,* the altar, and the *Menorah* all had to be rededicated because they had been defiled by the Greeks, this leniency could not be relied upon.

The oil used for rededicating the *Menorah* had to be ritually pure: the source of spiritual light for our world cannot be established through divine service that is acceptable only after the fact. On the contrary, the rededication of the *Beis HaMikdash* requires divine service of the highest level attainable. This was achieved by the *mesirus nefesh* ("self-sacrifice") of the Maccabees in their struggle for purity.

Making Our World a Dwelling Place for G-d

To the superficial observer, our world appears to function as an utterly physical entity, with no obvious connection to G-dliness or spirituality. This is the case because G-d desired "a dwelling in the lower worlds,"[7] meaning that He wanted His presence to be revealed in a setting where, by nature, He is not recognized.

---

5. *Zevachim* 22b; *Rambam, Hilchos Bias HaMikdash* 4:9.
6. *Gilyonei HaShas, Shabbos* 21b. See also the above essay on "The Message of the Chanukah Lights," which offers an alternative resolution to this question.
7. *Midrash Tanchuma, Parshas Bechukosai,* sec. 3; cited in *Tanya,* chs. 33 and 36.

The very nature of the material framework which He created obscures spiritual awareness and breeds self-concern. A
radical change, the introduction of a new approach to existence, is necessary for the world to serve as a dwelling place
for G-d.[8]

The construction of the Sanctuary and later, the *Beis
HaMikdash,* ushered in this new approach, for these struc-
tures served as "dwelling places for G-d," places where His
presence was openly revealed.[9] To inaugurate a structure of
this type, a heightened level of divine service is required; this
is what is meant by *chinuch* — "dedication".

A Focus on Children

Chinuch, as has been mentioned, also means "education".
The introduction of radical changes also takes place in the
education of a child. Education is not intended to merely enable the child to progress somewhat within his existing cog-
nitive framework, but to introduce him to new approaches
and effect pervasive changes in his nature.

For this reason, at the beginning of his formal education
(and at the introduction of each new stage in his development), the child is given presents which, like the additional
sacrifices offered to dedicate the altar, will stimulate his
growth[10] throughout this lifelong endeavor. In the spirit of
Chanukah,[11] he will "always advance higher in holy matters."
This, too, is the motivation underlying the cherished custom

---

8. See *Likkutei Sichos,* Vol. VI, *Parshas Shmos.*
9. Moreover, the physical substance of the world itself was included in G-d's dwelling,
    as is reflected in the change in its halachic status. From the time an article was con-
    secrated for use in the Sanctuary or the *Beis HaMikdash,* it could not be used for
    mundane purposes.
10. See the *Rambam's* Commentary to the *Mishnah (Sanhedrin* 10:1); *Or HaTorah* on
    Chanukah, pp. 299b, 934b.
11. *Shabbos, loc. cit.* See the explanation in the above essay on "The Message of the
    Chanukah Lights."

of giving children the gifts of pocket money known as "Chanukah *gelt.*"[12]

To Dedicate the World

"Educate a youth according to his way; even when he grows old, he will not depart from it."[13] The points outlined above remain relevant as youths mature and start homes of their own, for every Jewish home is a "sanctuary in microcosm"[14] which must be dedicated to serve as a source for the diffusion of Divine light.

Through our efforts in the study of Torah, in the service of prayer, and in giving *tzedakah,* we continuously spread G-dly light throughout the entire world. Chanukah in particular reminds us to spread the "lamp of a *mitzvah* and the light of the Torah,"[15] even when darkness appears to envelop our surroundings.

Chanukah thus represents "the dedication of the world,"[16] for the world was created for the sake of the Torah,[17] and the miracles of Chanukah make it possible for this purpose to be fulfilled. Thus, as the light of Chanukah spreads throughout the world, we become conscious that the world is G-d's dwelling place, and thereby hasten the coming of the Redemption, when we will dedicate the Third *Beis HaMikdash.* May this take place in the immediate future.

---

12. *HaYom Yom,* entry for 28 Kislev. The importance of this custom may be seen in the preference for giving children Chanukah *gelt* several times during Chanukah. See *Hisvaaduyos 5747,* Vol. 2, p. 123, footnote 23 and sources cited there; see also the *Sichah* of 22 Kislev, 5749.
13. *Mishlei* 22:6.
14. Cf. *Megillah* 29a. See the essay entitled "Every Home a Chabad House" (*Sichos In English,* Vol. 34, pp. 39-48.)
15. *Mishlei* 6:23.
16. *Shelah, Torah SheBichsav,* p. 301b (in the Amsterdam edition).
17. *Rashi* on *Bereishis* 1:1.

The Tenth of Teves

SUPPORT FOR JERUSALEM

Adapted from Likkutei Sichos,
Vol. XXV, p. 268;
the *Sichos* of Asarah BeTeves,
5739, 5745

"The Essence of this Day"

The fast of the Tenth of Teves is marked by a halachic stringency greater than that of all the other commemorative fasts. When any of those fasts fall on *Shabbos*, they are postponed to the following day. If, however, the Tenth of Teves were to fall on *Shabbos*,[1] then according to certain authorities,[2] we would be required to fast, even though this would prevent us from fulfilling the *mitzvah* of *oneg Shabbos* ("delighting in the Sabbath").

This unique status is based on the verse,[3] "*On this very day,* the King of Babylon laid siege to Jerusalem." This verse establishes an equivalence between the Tenth of Teves and Yom Kippur, about which it is written,[4] "And a person who does not afflict himself *on this very day....*" Just as the fasting of Yom Kippur is observed even on *Shabbos*, the fasting of the Tenth of Teves would be observed on *Shabbos*, if necessary.[5]

---

1. According to the fixed calendar which we use at present, this is impossible.
2. Avudraham, *Hilchos Taaniyos,* cited by the *Beis Yosef (Orach Chayim* 550).
3. *Yechezkel* 24:2. Moreover, the verse begins, "Son of man, write down the name of this day, the essence of this day...."
4. *Vayikra* 23:27.
5. Like Yom Kippur, this fast too occurs on the tenth of the month; cf. *(Vayikra* 27:32): "The tenth shall be holy." Teves, moreover, is the tenth month of the year (counting from Nissan), and the fast is referred to *(Zechariah* 8:19) as "the fast of the tenth [month]."

The First Stage of a Sequence

The Tenth of Teves commemorates the beginning of Nebuchadnezzar's siege of Jerusalem, the first stage in the sequence of events which led to the destruction of the city. The events that followed, the breaching of the city's walls during the month of Tammuz,[6] and the destruction of the *Beis HaMikdash* on Tishah BeAv, could not have taken place had the city not been besieged.

The first stage of any process contains the potential for all its subsequent stages. The tragic nature of the events commemorated by the other fasts may exceed that of the Tenth of Teves, but since the siege of Jerusalem initiated the sequence of events leading to the city's destruction, the Tenth of Teves is marked by greater severity.

A Missed Opportunity

All events, even those which appear to be tragic, have holy roots. Seen from this perspective, a calamity like the siege of Jerusalem indicates that the intense Divine energy invested was intended to produce a positive result. However, because of a deficiency in their service of G-d, the Jewish people failed to take advantage of this opportunity, and this brought about the ensuing tragedy.[7]

This concept is alluded to in the Hebrew words of the Biblical verse cited above, *samach melech Bavel* ("the King of Babylon laid siege"). The Hebrew verb *samach* usually means

---

6. According to most opinions, the walls of Jerusalem were breached (before the First Destruction) on the ninth of Tammuz (*Rosh HaShanah* 18b). There are, however, opinions (see *Jerusalem Talmud, Taanis* 4:5 and the Glosses of Rabbeinu Nissim and the *Ritva* to *Rosh HaShanah*) which maintain that then, too, the walls of Jerusalem were breached on the seventeenth of the month, the date on which this calamity occurred before the Second Destruction.

7. That a tragedy possesses an elevated source is illustrated by the following analogy: When a stone wall collapses, the higher the position of a stone the further away will it fall (*Likkutei Torah, Parshas Re'eh*, p. 19c).

"support" and has a positive connotation.[8] This may be understood as an indication that the siege of Jerusalem could have led to a positive outcome.

The possibility for such an outcome may be seen from an earlier siege of Jerusalem. The siege laid by Sennacherib, King of Assyria, was even more severe than that of Nebuchadnezzar.[9] Faced with impending disaster, King Chizkiyahu prayed to G-d with sincere *teshuvah*. His prayer brought about a miraculous victory, in which the danger was averted in a single night.[10] Moreover, this victory had spiritual implications: "G-d desired to make Chizkiyahu *Mashiach*."[11]

G-d's intention in allowing Nebuchadnezzar's siege of Jerusalem to take place was to awaken the people spiritually. This would have created "support" for the city, strengthening it against its foes, and hastening the coming of the Redemption.

Unrestrained Love

The positive intention at the heart of these national calamities is reflected in our commemoration of them, for the purpose of the commemorative fasts is not fasting *per se,* but rather the repentance of the Jewish people.[12] Ultimately, this positive intention will blossom forth in the Era of the Redemption when, as the *Rambam* writes,[13] "All these [commemorative] fasts will be nullified;... indeed,... they will

---

8. Cf. *Tehillim* 145:14, *Somech HaShem lechol hanoflim* — "G-d supports all those who fall."
9. Commenting on *Yeshayahu* 10:32, *Rashi* states that had Sennacherib attacked Jerusalem, he would have conquered it in a single day. Nebuchadnezzar, by contrast, was forced to besiege the city for an extended period.
10. See *II Melachim* 19:35; see also *Tanna dvei Eliyahu,* ch. 7.
11. *Sanhedrin* 94a.
12. *Rambam, Mishneh Torah, Hilchos Taaniyos* 5:1.
13. *Loc. cit.* 5:19.

be transformed into holidays and days of rejoicing and celebration."

As a prooftext, the *Rambam* cites the prophecy:[14] "Thus declares the L-rd of Hosts, 'The fast of the fourth [month], the fast of the fifth [month], the fast of the seventh [month], and the fast of the tenth [month], will be [times of] happiness and celebration and festivals for the House of Judah. Love truth and peace!' "

By including the concluding admonition ("Love truth and peace!"), the *Rambam* points out the approach necessary to precipitate the transformation of the fasts into days of celebration. Our Sages explain[15] that the destruction of Jerusalem and the exile of our people came about because of unwarranted hatred.[16] Displaying unrestrained love for our fellow man, spreading "truth and peace," will erase the reason for the exile, and then the exile itself will come to an end.

This concept is particularly relevant to the Tenth of Teves and indeed is reflected in the events commemorated by that day. For, as the result of a siege, all the inhabitants of a city are prevented from going about their personal business and are joined together as a single collective entity.[17]

Since, as stated above, the fast of the Tenth of Teves commemorates the beginning of the process of Jerusalem's

---

14. *Zechariah, loc. cit.*
15. *Yoma* 9b; *Gittin* 55b.
16. Unwarranted hatred is given as a reason for the destruction of the second *Beis HaMikdash* and the consequent present exile. Although Zechariah is referring to fasts that were instituted in connection with the destruction of the First *Beis HaMikdash*, it is not until the end of the present exile and the coming of the Redemption that his prophecy, the transformation of the fasts into days of rejoicing, will be realized.

    In addition, there is a connection between unwarranted hatred and the destruction of the First *Beis HaMikdash* as well, for as is taught in *Bereishis Rabbah* 38:6, were the unity of the Jewish people to be absolute, no foe could overcome them.
17. Moreover, the fact that the beleaguered people were confined within Jerusalem is particularly significant for, as indicated by *Tehillim* 122:3 (as interpreted by the *Jerusalem Talmud, Chagigah* 3:6), the city of Jerusalem has a unique tendency to encourage unity.

destruction, its impact is of broader scope than is the impact of the other commemorative fasts. Accordingly, the *teshuvah* which its commemoration spurs is particularly potent in hastening the coming of the Redemption. This will initiate an era when[18] "Jerusalem will be settled like an open city, because of the multitude of people and cattle it contains... and I... will be a wall of fire around her." May this take place in the immediate future.

---

18. *Zechariah* 2:8-9.

Yud Shvat

A LEGACY OF SELF-SACRIFICE

Adapted from *Likkutei Sichos*,
Vol. XVIII, *Parshas Chukas-Balak*
and *Yud-Beis* Tammuz;
and the *Sichos* of *Shabbos Parshas Beshallach*, 5751

A Time for Focus

Yud Shvat (the Tenth of Shvat) is the Previous Rebbe's *yahrzeit*, the anniversary of his passing. On the day of a *tzaddik's* passing, "all his effort... for which he toiled throughout his life... becomes revealed and radiates downward... at the time of his passing."[1] Accordingly, *Yud* Shvat is an appropriate day to focus on the message of the Previous Rebbe's life, for every year, these same spiritual qualities are revealed on this anniversary.[2]

This revelation affects all of "his children, the work of his hands," those who "will walk in his paths for eternity."[3] This is particularly true in regard to the *yahrzeit* of a *nasi*, a leader of the Jewish people. For a *nasi* is connected to every member of his generation;[4] as *Rashi* states,[5] "The *nasi* is the entire people."

The divine service of every man, but particularly that of a *tzaddik* and *nasi*, is multifaceted. Nevertheless, in considering the Previous Rebbe's divine service as a whole, there is one quality that stands out distinctly, and which enhances the

---

1.   *Tanya, Iggeres HaKodesh*, Epistle 28.
2.   See *Ramaz* in *Sefer Tikkun Shovavim*, cited and explained in *Lev David*, ch. 29; see also *Likkutei Sichos*, Vol. XVI, p. 139, footnote 1.
3.   See *Tanya, Iggeres HaKodesh*, Epistle 27.
4.   See *Tanya*, ch. 2.
5.   On *Bamidbar* 21:23.

nature of all his other contributions, namely, his unbounded *mesirus nefesh* ("self sacrifice").

The Previous Rebbe's *mesirus nefesh* was not limited to a particular situation or mode of expression. Despite the radically differing settings in which he lived and the varied nature of the obstacles with which he was confronted, he showed an unceasing commitment to the well-being of his fellow Jews, and to their connection with their Torah heritage.

Challenging the Iron Fist

His resolution and unbounded concern may be seen in his responses to three challenges that marked the three decades during which he served as leader of the *Chabad* chassidic movement. The Previous Rebbe assumed the mantle of leadership in 5680 (1920). At that time, the majority of the *Chabad* community — and the largest Jewish population worldwide — was located in the Soviet Union, exposed to the full brunt of the Communist effort to stamp out religious practice.

For the Previous Rebbe, every day presented a life-and-death struggle to maintain the observance of Torah throughout the country. He dispatched rabbis and *shochtim* to communities throughout the land, built *mikvaos,* and most important — and most fiercely opposed by the Communist regime — he established an extensive network of underground *chadarim* and *yeshivos* to educate Jewish youth. (This network continued to operate for decades, until the Glasnost allowed these schools to emerge into the light of day.)

The Previous Rebbe was arrested several times for "counter-revolutionary" activities. At one point, he was sentenced to death; only through international intervention and a series of miracles was the sentence averted.[6] The most diffi-

---

6.   *Sefer HaToldos* of the Previous Rebbe, Vol. III, p. 191ff.

cult part of the Rebbe's situation, however, was the threat to his followers who joined him in risking their lives for these goals. Whenever one of his followers was exiled to Siberia for teaching young children, the Previous Rebbe had to shoulder the responsibility of sending a replacement with the full knowledge of the danger awaiting him.

In the Twilight Before the Night

The Rebbe Rayatz was forced to leave Russia in 5688 (1928). For the next few years, he established his base in Riga. Although he visited several Jewish communities throughout the world during this time, his energies were still primarily focused on Russia and the operation of the chassidic movement there.

In the summer of 5693 (1933), he settled in Poland. There, he was confronted by challenges of a different nature. Although there were no political obstacles to the spread of Jewish education or practice, the lack of resources presented difficulties which were compounded by the fact that the leaders of the local Jewish community did not understand his approach.

The Previous Rebbe did not allow these impediments to stand in the way of his efforts. With relentless energy, he established a chain of *yeshivos* and *chadarim* that enabled thousands of youth to devote themselves to the study of Torah. These activities continued until they were halted by the Nazi invasion. Together with thousands of other Jews, the Previous Rebbe spent the High Holidays of 5700 (1939) in bomb shelters in Warsaw. Shortly thereafter, on the last passenger ship to leave, he set out for the United States.

"America is No Different"

Immediately upon his arrival, he announced that he had come not for his personal benefit, but to prove that "America is no different."[7] The spiritual vitality that had nurtured Jewish life in Eastern Europe could be transplanted to the American continent. Though its manner of expression might change, the traditional devotion to the Torah's teachings and the observance of the *mitzvos* would not.

Physically broken by the ravages of ill-health and Soviet interrogators, the Previous Rebbe could have retired to a more private life, leading his own small group of followers. Instead, he revolutionized American Judaism. Every single area of American Jewish life — day schools, *kashrus,* Jewish publishing, *yeshivah* study, and the beginnings of the *baal teshuvah* movement — was radically influenced by his activities.

His ability to practice *mesirus nefesh* in these three very different situations indicates that this quality was of his essence. Himself the epitome of *mesirus nefesh,* he was able to inspire others likewise.

Continually Advancing — and with Joy

The very name Yosef Yitzchak speaks volumes about the Rebbe Rayatz.

In Hebrew, Yosef (יוסף) means "increase". The Previous Rebbe's *mesirus nefesh* constantly impelled him to further commitment and increased activity. Moreover, the name Yosef was first given in the verse,[8] "May G-d *add on (yosef)* to me *another son (ben acher)."* Implicit in this verse is the ability of Yosef to transform a person who has hitherto been *acher*

---

7.   *Sefer HaSichos 5703,* p. 147; *Igros Kodesh* (Letters) of the Rebbe Rayatz, Vol. .VII, p. 336.
8.   *Bereishis* 30:24.

("another" — estranged from his Jewish roots) into the closeness of *ben* ("a son"). This ability was exemplified by the Previous Rebbe, who inspired countless Jews to return to Jewish practice.

The name Yitzchak was first given in the verse,[9] "Whoever hears *will laugh* (*yitzchak*) with me." Joy should be radiated to the point that "whoever hears," even someone who does not consciously intend to hear, "will laugh with me."

In keeping with this verse, the Previous Rebbe possessed a unique ability to impart happiness to others. Even when he was physically broken, the atmosphere around him was never one of despair. Quite the contrary, he radiated joy.

Both these names share a connection to the Redemption. The name Yosef is associated with the verse,[10] "G-d *will again* (*yosif*) extend His hand... to take possession of the remnant of His people." The joy inspired by the name Yitzchak anticipates the overwhelming joy our people will experience at the Redemption, as it is written,[11] "Then will our mouths be filled with laughter." May this take place in the immediate future.

---

9. *Op. cit.* 21:6.
10. *Yeshayahu* 11:11.
11. *Tehillim* 126:2.

TOWARDS A NEW DAWN

The essay that follows differs from the others in this series in that it does not adapt one of the talks of the Rebbe *Shlita*. For obvious reasons, the Rebbe himself has not highlighted the aspect of *Yud* Shvat which is the focus of this essay. We, however, could not omit this essay from the series, because for many chassidim today, it describes the most significant aspect of *Yud* Shvat. We have therefore woven together several of the talks of the Rebbe *Shlita* from different occasions to create an original composition with the intention of communicating feelings which many share.

"The Sun Rises and the Sun Sets"

In one of his public talks regarding *Beis* Nissan,[1] the *yahrzeit* of the Rebbe Rashab, the Rebbe *Shlita* pointed out that there are two aspects to the passing of the Rebbe Rashab. The first is that "all his effort... for which he toiled throughout his life... becomes revealed and radiates downward... at the time of his passing."[2] The second is that this date marks the beginning of the *nesius* of the Rebbe Rayatz, the date on which he assumed the responsibilities of leadership as Rebbe.

On the verse,[3] "The sun rises and the sun sets," our Sages comment[4] that a righteous man will not pass away until another righteous man of equal stature arises to take his

---

1.   *Sefer HaSichos 5748*, Vol. I, p. 347.
2.   *Tanya, Iggeres HaKodesh*, Epistle 28; see also the above essay entitled "A Legacy of Self-Sacrifice."
3.   *Koheles* 1:5.
4.   *Yoma* 38b; *Koheles Rabbah* on the above verse.

place. Our Sages also point out[5] that G-d did not delay the
death of King David, because the time had come for his son
Shlomo to reign, and the reign of one king should not
impinge upon the reign of another.

The Rebbe *Shlita* has explained that while both aspects of
Beis Nissan are significant, it is the assumption of the *nesius*
by the Rebbe Rayatz that is of paramount relevance to us. The
same surely applies to *Yud* Shvat,[6] the date which marks both
the *yahrzeit* of the Rebbe Rayatz, and the ascent of the Rebbe
Shlita to the *nesius*. Without minimizing the weight of the
former aspect of *Yud* Shvat, for many chassidim today the
assumption of the *nesius* by the Rebbe *Shlita* is the primary
focus of the day.

For the Divine Presence to Dwell among Mortals

In the first *maamar* the Rebbe *Shlita* delivered,[7] he outlined his goals for our generation:

> We are in the midst of the period called *ikvesa
> diMeshicha* (i.e., the time when the approaching foot-
> steps of *Mashiach* can be heard). Indeed, we are at the
> conclusion of this period. Our task is to complete the
> process of drawing down the Divine Presence... so
> that it should rest within our lowly world.

---

5. *Shabbos* 30a.
6. In this context, we can apply the Baal Shem Tov's interpretation of the expression
of the *Mishnah* (*Avos* 3:16), "The collectors... exact payment from man with or
without his knowledge." The Baal Shem Tov explains (*Likkutei Maharan*, sec. 113)
that since every Jew's soul is "an actual part of G-d from above" (*Tanya*, ch. 2), it is
impossible for any being, even the angels of the Heavenly Court, to judge him.

   How then is "payment exacted"? Divine Providence gives the person the opportunity, in his casual discussions with a friend or the like, to judge a colleague who
has performed a similar deed. Afterwards, the judgment made "with his knowledge" about a colleague is then "without his knowledge" applied to him himself by
the Heavenly Court (*Likkutei Sichos*, Vol. IV, p. 1207). Similarly, in the case at
hand, the statements made by the Rebbe *Shlita* about *Beis* Nissan may be regarded
as applicable to *Yud* Shvat.
7. *Basi LeGani 5711*, sec. 3.

In the talks he delivered on the same occasion,[8] the Rebbe *Shlita* explained that though Moshe could have constructed the entire Sanctuary himself, he refrained from doing so, in order to enable the entire Jewish people to participate in this endeavor. Similarly, the Rebbe *Shlita* continued, the Rebbeim of past generations did not want the campaign to bring *Mashiach* to be their private undertaking, but rather an effort shared by the Jewish people as a whole, and by each individual Jew.

This goal has been at the heart of the efforts of the Rebbe *Shlita* throughout his leadership of the *Chabad* chassidic movement for more than four decades. During this period, he has transformed *Chabad*-Lubavitch into a vast international movement with farflung influence and a veritable kaleidoscope of activities — all of which, directly or indirectly, share a single purpose, to hasten the coming of the Era of the Redemption.

To Accept Mashiach

A person who has always conceived of the coming of *Mashiach* as an abstract idea may not appreciate what this means in actual fact. The focus of the Rebbe *Shlita* has constantly been on the concrete reality — that *Mashiach* actually come and inaugurate a new era for the world.

This has been the center of Lubavitch attention, especially since the eve of the 28th of Nissan, 5751. On that evening, in the midst of what had begun as a scholarly discussion of the distinct spiritual potentials of the current year, month, and date, the Rebbe turned to his followers with a cry from the heart:[9]

> What more can I do to motivate the entire Jewish people to clamor and cry out, and thus actually bring

8. *Likkutei Sichos,* Vol. II, p. 501.
9. *Sound the Great Shofar* (Kehot, N.Y., 5752), pp. 35-36.

about the coming of *Mashiach?*... All that I can possibly do is give the matter over to you. Now, do everything you can do to bring *Mashiach,* here and now, immediately.... I have done whatever I can; from now on you must do whatever you can.

As the Rebbe *Shlita* pointed out in the following months, these efforts reflected the unique spiritual climate of our times:[10]

> We are standing on the threshold of the future Redemption. *Mashiach's* coming is no longer a dream of the distant future, but an imminent reality which will very shortly become fully manifest.

With increasing energy, the Rebbe *Shlita* continued to develop this theme in the months that followed:[11]

> Our Sages[12] have described the Redemption as a feast. To speak in terms of this analogy,[13] the table has already been set, everything has been served, we are sitting at the table together with *Mashiach.* All we need to do is open our eyes....

> Our Sages[14] describe *Mashiach* as waiting anxiously to come. In previous generations, however, his coming was delayed by the fact that the Jewish people had not completed the tasks expected of them. Now, however, those tasks have been accomplished; there is nothing lacking. All we have to do is accept *Mashiach.*

---

10. *Ibid.* p. 47.
11. *Ibid.* pp. 112-113.
12. *Pesachim* 119b.
13. As is obvious from the comments of the *Ramban (Shaar HaGemul)* and *Raavad* on the statements of the *Rambam* in *Hilchos Teshuvah* 8:4, the intent is that this will be an actual feast. Nevertheless, as is evident from the discussion of the subject in Rabbinic sources, every detail of this feast also has profound allegorical significance.
14. *Sanhedrin* 98a.

On *Yud* Shvat, when a chassid contemplates his relationship with the Rebbe *Shlita,* and the course of action this relationship should inspire, it is clear that his energies should be directed to one goal — making the world conscious of *Mashiach* and creating an environment in which his mission can be fulfilled. May this take place in the immediate future.

The New Year of Trees

WHY WE CELEBRATE
THE NEW YEAR OF TREES

Adapted from *Likkutei Sichos*,
Vol. VI, p. 308-309;
Vol. XXIV, p. 115 ff.

"Is Man a Tree of the Field?"

Tu BiShvat, "the New Year of the Trees,"[1] has its own customs,[2] which our Rabbis[3] associate with the phrase,[4] "Is man a tree of the field?" Because the tree-metaphor is so fundamental to our divine service, we celebrate the New Year of the Trees.

A tree may be divided into three parts: (a) roots; (b) trunk, branches and leaves; and (c) fruit. Though the roots of a tree are not visible, they serve two vital functions: they support the tree, enabling it to withstand strong winds, and they deliver most of its nourishment. The trunk, branches and leaves constitute the bulk of the tree's body, reflect its growth, and make the tree attractive to the onlooker — but they are not its ultimate purpose. It is the fruit[5] that benefits others and contains the seeds which bear the species' promise for posterity.

---

1. *Rosh HaShanah* 1:1; *Shulchan Aruch, Orach Chayim* 131:6.
2. *Magen Avraham* 131:16; see also *Pri Etz Hadar*, which mentions several Kabbalistic customs associated with this date.
3. *Likkutei Maharich*, Vol. III, *Minhagei Shvat*.
4. *Devarim* 20:19.
5. The centrality of a tree's the fruit is indicated by the way the Torah records the creation of the trees (*Bereishis* 1:11): "Let the earth give forth... fruit trees, that produce their own species of fruit."

These components of the tree symbolize aspects of our personalities. The roots represent faith, the spiritual quality which connects man to G-d, the source of his nourishment. As a person develops spiritually, he learns to rely on his strong foundations of faith for support.

The trunk, branches and leaves represent our study of Torah, observance of the *mitzvos,* and the expression of Jewish values in our daily conduct. These enable a person to develop himself and they generate an inner beauty which makes him attractive to others.

The ultimate fulfillment of a person, however, is his fruits. These are his involvements — first with his own family, the seeds he has planted, but also with the people around him. Through his efforts to become involved with others, one tree can bring another into being. For example, a person might inspire a colleague to emulate his example and establish a foundation of faith, grow in the study of Torah and the observance of *mitzvos,* and ultimately take his turn at reaching out to others with sincere concern.

Constant Growth

Men and trees are linked by more than merely structural parallels. The Hebrew word describing the plant kingdom, צומח, also means "growth". On one hand, this name reflects a deficiency; it is given to the plant kingdom, because growth is one of the few signs of life that plants exhibit. On the other hand, there is something unique about the growth of plants. As opposed to animals or humans, whose physical growth ceases at a particular age, plants continually grow; their life and growth are intrinsically related. This is particularly true of trees, which rise heavenward to great heights.

This should likewise be true of us. Though our physical growth may cease, we should strive to continue growing intellectually and spiritually, never ceasing to develop.

Rooted in the Source

Though a plant continually grows upward, in contrast to animals and humans, which move freely, it must remain firmly rooted in its source of nourishment, the earth.[6] As a Jew is continually growing, he too must remain connected to his roots, his Torah heritage. Most people need to spend most of their time in occupations and concerns that are beyond the immediate sphere of Torah. Under these circumstances, we can only flourish if our faith keeps us firmly rooted to our Torah heritage.

Furthermore, unlike other plants, trees not only remain alive throughout the year and endure its changes of climate, but they continue to grow. This quality can teach us to endeavor to see every situation as potentially contributing to our growth. We need to develop the flexibility and the resilience that enable us to respond positively to change.

As Seedlings Grow and Thrive

Tu BiShvat, like other Jewish holidays, has a special meaning for children, who fulfill the custom of eating Tu BiShvat fruits with gusto. The connection between Tu BiShvat and children brings to mind another lesson applicable to our lives. Just as a small improvement in a seedling produces a greatly improved tree, so too, a small improvement in a child's education can affect him throughout his entire life thereafter.

Our prophets use the metaphor of trees to describe the Jewish people in their ultimate state of fulfillment, the Era of the Redemption:[7] "In days to come, Yaakov will take root;

---

6. Though a fish must also remain continually connected to its source of nourishment (the water), its entire body must remain inseparably in its source. A plant, by contrast, emerges from its source and grows above the earth while maintaining a constant bond with it.
7. *Yeshayahu* 27:6.

Yisrael will blossom and bud, and will cover the face of the earth with fruit." The coming of *Mashiach*[8] is described similarly: "A shoot shall emerge from the stem of Yishai, and a branch shall grow out from his roots." May these prophecies be fulfilled in the immediate future.

---

8. *Ibid.* 11:1.

Glossary
and Biographical Index

GLOSSARY AND BIOGRAPHICAL INDEX

Aharon: Aaron, the first High Priest

Akiva, Rabbi: one of the foremost sages of the Talmudic period, unlearned until the age of 40, whose ardent efforts enabled him to serve as a major figure in the transmission of the Torah tradition

Alter Rebbe, the (lit., "the Old Rebbe"): Rabbi Shneur Zalman of Liadi (1745-1812), the founder of the *Chabad-*Lubavitch trend within the chassidic movement; author of the *Tanya,* a classic text of the chassidic tradition, and *Shulchan Aruch HaRav,* a classic legal code

amcha Yidden: plain, honest folk

avodah (lit., "service"): formerly, the sacrificial service in the Temple, and later, the service of prayer instituted in its stead

Avraham Avinu (lit., "our father Abraham"): the Patriarch Abraham

AriZal (lit., "the lion of blessed memory"): R. Isaac Luria (1534-1572), one of the leading Kabbalistic* luminaries

Baal Shem Tov, the (lit., "Master of the Good Name"): Rabbi Yisrael ben Eliezer (1698-1760), founder of Chassidism

baal teshuvah (lit. "master of return"): a person who turns to G-d in repentance, after willful or unknowing transgression of the Torah's commandments

Beis HaMikdash: the (First or Second) Temple in Jerusalem

Chabad (acronym for the Hebrew words meaning "wisdom, under-standing, and knowledge"): the approach to Chassidism which filters its spiritual and emotional power through the intellect; a synonym for *Chabad* is *Lubavitch, the name of the town where this movement originally flourished

Chai Elul (lit., "the Eighteenth of Elul"): the birthday of both the Baal Shem Tov (1698) and the Alter Rebbe (1745)

Chanukah (lit., "dedication"): eight-day festival beginning 25 Kislev, commemorating the Maccabees' rededication of the Temple in the second century B.C.E., and marked by the kindling of lights

Chassidus: chassidic thought

chinuch: (lit. "dedication" or "education")

Chizkiyahu: Hezekiah, one of the last righteous kings in the First Temple Period

Elul: the sixth month of the Jewish year when counting from Nissan (or the twelfth when counting from Tishrei); a month devoted to repentance and soul-searching in preparation for the Days of Awe

Eretz Yisrael: the Land of Israel

gematria: the Hebrew letters also serve as numerals. Since G-d created the world through speech, the numerical equivalence between words indicates an intrinsic connection

Haftorah (lit., "the final passage"): the passage from the Prophets read in the synagogue after the conclusion of the Torah reading

Haggadah (lit., "telling"): the text from which the *Seder service is conducted on the first two nights of Passover (outside of *Eretz Yisrael,* and in *Eretz Yisrael* on the first night only)

Halachah (pl., *halachos*): (a) the body of Torah law; (b) a particular law

Holy of Holies: the inner chamber of the Temple where the Divine Presence was revealed. In the First Temple, it contained the Holy Ark

Kabbalah (lit., "received tradition"): the Jewish mystical tradition

kabbalas ol (lit., "the acceptance of [G-d's] yoke"): an unswerving, selfless commitment to carrying out the Will of G-d

Kislev: the ninth month of the Jewish year when counting from Nissan (or the third when counting from Tishrei)

Levi Yitzchak of Berditchev, Rabbi: one of the foremost disciples of the Maggid of Mezritch; renowned for his all-encompassing love and care for the Jewish people and for every individual Jew

Likkutei Dibburim: a selection of the public talks of the sixth Lubavitcher Rebbe, Rabbi Yosef Yitzchak Schneersohn (see *Previous Rebbe)

Likkutei Torah: a collection of chassidic discourses by Rabbi Shneur Zalman of Liadi (see *Alter Rebbe)

Lubavitch: name of the village in White Russia which for a century was the home of the Rebbeim of *Chabad, and which is hence used as a name for the movement

maamar: a formal chassidic discourse

Maccabees: the sons of Mattisyahu the priest who inspired the revolt against the Syrian-Greek rulers of *Eretz Yisrael* which culminated in the *Chanukah miracle

machzor: the special prayer book used on holidays

Maggid of Mezritch (lit., "the preacher of Mezritch"): R. Dov Ber (d. 1772), disciple and successor of the *Baal Shem Tov; mentor of the *Alter Rebbe

Mashiach (lit., "the anointed one"): the Messiah

matzah: the unleavened bread eaten on Passover (see *Pesach)

Megillah (lit., "scroll"): the Biblical book of *Esther;* the parchment scroll on which that book is recorded

menorah: the golden candelabrum lit in the Temple

mesirus nefesh (lit., "sacrifice of the soul"): the willingness to sacrifice oneself, either through martyrdom, or through a selfless life, for the sake of the Torah and its commandments

Midrash: classical collection of the Sages' homiletical teachings on the Bible

Mishnah: the germinal statements of law elucidated by the *Gemara,* together with which they constitute the *Talmud*

Mitteler Rebbe, the (lit., "the Middle Rebbe"; Yid.): R. Dov Ber (1773-1827), son and successor of the *Alter Rebbe

mitzvah (pl., *mitzvos;* lit., "command"): a religious obligation; one of the Torah's 613 Commandments

Moshe Rabbeinu (lit., "Moses our Teacher"): the "father of the prophets," who redeemed the Jews from Egypt and brought them to the revelation at Mount Sinai

Nasi: (a) in Biblical times, the head of any one of the Twelve Tribes; (b) in later generations, the civil and/or spiritual head of the Jewish community at large

Neilah (lit., "locking"): the fifth prayer service recited before the conclusion of Yom Kippur, when the gates of heaven are being locked

nigleh (lit., "the revealed [knowledge]"): the study of Jewish law as reflected in the Talmud, and in the works of the subsequent commentators and codifiers

Nissan: the first month of the Jewish year according to certain reckonings, or the seventh when counting the months from Tishrei; the month of the Exodus from Egypt

"Pardes" (lit., "orchard"): the metaphorical term used to refer to (a) the four levels of Torah interpretation: *pshat* (the literal meaning of the text), *remez* (its allusions), *derush* (the homilies that can be derived from it), and *sod* (its mystical secrets); (b) more particularly, the study and experience of those mystical secrets

Parshah: portion of the Torah read publicly every week

Parshas...: the *Parshah* of [a certain *Shabbos* or festive occasion]

Pesach: Passover, seven-day festival beginning on 15 Nissan, commemorating the Exodus from Egypt

pnimiyus HaTorah (lit., "the inner dimension of [the Torah]"): the mystical dimension of Torah study

Pesach Sheni (lit., "the second Passover"): opportunity given to certain persons who were unable to offer the Paschal sacrifice to do so one month later, on 14 Iyar

Previous Rebbe, the: Rabbi Yosef Yitzchak Schneersohn (1880-1950; also known by the acronym of his name as the Rebbe Rayatz), the sixth Lubavitcher Rebbe, who headed the movement's active resistance against the Communist suppression of religion in Soviet Russia and who transferred the movement to the US during World War II

Purim (lit., "lots"): one-day festival falling on 14 Adar and commemorating the miraculous salvation of the Jews of the Persian Empire in the fourth century B.C.E.

Rambam (acronym for Rabbi Moshe ben Maimon; 1135-1204): Maimonides, one of the foremost Jewish thinkers of the Middle Ages; his *Mishneh Torah* is one of the pillars of Jewish law, and his *Guide to the Perplexed,* one of the classics of Jewish philosophy

Rashi (acronym for Rabbi Shlomo Yitzchaki; 1040-1105): the author of the foremost commentaries to the Torah and the *Talmud*

Rebbe (lit., "my teacher [or master]"): saintly Torah leader who serves as spiritual guide to a following of chassidim

Rebbe Maharash (acronym for *Moreinu* ("Our teacher") *HaRav* Shmuel): R. Shmuel Schneersohn of Lubavitch (1834-1882); the son and successor of the *Tzemach Tzedek

Rebbe Rashab: (acronym for Rabbi Sholom DovBer): Rabbi Sholom DovBer Schneersohn (1860-1920), the son and successor of the *Rebbe Maharash, who founded the Tomchei Temimim Yeshivah in Lubavitch in 1897

Rosh HaShanah (lit., "head of the year"): the New Year festival, falling on 1 and 2 Tishrei

Sanhedrin: the High Court of 71 sages in Jerusalem which served as the supreme authority on Jewish law

Shabbos: the Sabbath

Shavuos (lit., "weeks"): festival commemorating the Giving of the Torah at Sinai, in *Eretz Yisrael* falling on 6 Sivan, and in the Diaspora on 6-7 Sivan

Shechinah: the Divine Presence

Shlita: an acronym for the Hebrew words meaning: "May he live a long and good life"

Shlomo: King David's son and successor, who built the First Temple in the tenth century B.C.E.

Shmuel: the prophet Samuel

Shulchan Aruch: the standard Code of Jewish Law compiled by Rabbi Yosef Caro in the mid-sixteenth century

Shulchan Aruch HaRav (or "the Alter Rebbe's *Shulchan Aruch*") is the later edition compiled by the *Alter Rebbe

Shvat: the eleventh month of the Jewish year when counting from Nissan (or the fifth when counting from Tishrei)

Simchas Beis HaShoevah: the celebration which accompanied the water libation in the Temple on *Sukkos

Simchas Torah (lit., "the rejoicing of the Torah"): the final day (in *Eretz Yisrael,* the eighth day; in the diaspora, the ninth) of the festival of *Sukkos on which the annual cycle of Torah readings is completed; this event is celebrated with exuberant rejoicing

sukkah (lit., "booth"; pl., *sukkos*): a temporary dwelling in which we are commanded to live during the festival of *Sukkos

Sukkos (lit., "Booths"): seven-day festival (eight days in the Diaspora) beginning on 15 Tishrei, taking its name from the temporary dwelling in which one lives during this period

Tammuz: the fourth month of the Jewish year when counting from Nissan (or the tenth when counting from Tishrei)

Tanach: the Bible

Tanya: the classic text of *Chabad chassidic thought authored by the *Alter Rebbe

tefillin: small leather boxes each containing four Biblical passages which the Torah commands adult males to wear daily during morning prayers

Tehillim (lit., "praises"): the Book of *Psalms*

teshuvah (lit., "return [to G-d]"): repentance

Teves: the tenth month of the Jewish year when counting from Nissan (or the fourth when counting for Tishrei)

Thirteen Attributes of Mercy: G-d's boundless capacity for compassion, especially as expressed in the granting of atonement

Tishah BeAv (lit., "the Ninth of Av"): fast commemorating the Destruction of both the First and the Second Temple

Tishrei: the first month of the Jewish year according to certain reckonings, or the seventh when counting the months from Nissan; the month which includes *Rosh HaShanah, *Yom Kippur and *Sukkos

Tu BiShvat (lit., "the Fifteenth of Shvat"): "The New Year of the Trees," celebrated every year as a minor festival

tzaddik: righteous man

tzedakah: charity

Tzemach Tzedek: R. Menachem Mendel Schneersohn (1789-1866); son-in-law and successor of the Mitteler Rebbe; known by the title of the collection of Responsa which he authored

Ushpizin ("honored guests"): seven leading figures in Jewish history who make noncorporeal visits to our *sukkos* on the holiday of that name

VeAl HaNissim (lit., "And for the miracles"): the opening phrase of a passage included in the daily prayers and the grace after meals on Chanukah and Purim, thankfully acknowledging the miracles G-d wrought on those days

Yaakov Avinu: the Patriarch Jacob

yahrzeit (Yid.): the anniversary of a person's passing

yechidah: the highest of the five levels of the soul, the rung in which the soul is in absolute unity with G-d

Yechezkel: the prophet Ezekiel

Yehoshua: Joshua, the leader of the Jewish people after Moses

Yehudah: Judah

Yehudah HaNasi, Rabbi ("Rabbi Yehudah the Prince"): leader of the Jewish people in *Eretz Yisrael* shortly after the Destruction of the Second Temple; compiler of the *Mishnah

yeshivah: Rabbinical academy

Yetzer HaRa: the Evil Inclination

Yitzchak Avinu: the Patriarch Isaac

Yom Kippur: the Day of Atonement, fast day falling on 10 Tishrei and climaxing the Days of Awe

Yud-Beis Tammuz: the twelfth of Tammuz; the Previous Rebbe's birthday and the anniversary of his release from capital sentence and imprisonment in Soviet Russia in 1927

Yud Shvat (lit., "the Tenth of Shvat"): anniversary of the passing of the *Previous Rebbe in 1950

Yud-Tes Kislev (lit., "the Nineteenth of Kislev"): anniversary of the passing of the Maggid of Mezritch in 1772, and anniversary of the release from capital sentence of his disciple, the *Alter Rebbe, in 1798

Zohar (lit., "radiance"): the classic text of the *Kabbalah

לזכות

הוו"ח הרה"ת ר' **משה אהרן צבי** בן **מרים** שיחי'
וזוגתו מרת **העניא רבקה רות** בת **צפורה** שתחי'
ובנם **שלום אליעזר** שיחי'
וייס
שערמאן אוקס, קאליפורניא

שהקב"ה ימלא כל משאלות לבבם לטובה בגו"ר

♦

Dedicated by

Rabbi Moshe and Ruty שיחיו Weiss

Sherman Oaks, California

May the Almighty fulfill their hearts' desires
both materially and spiritually

הוצאת ספרים

קרני הוד תורה

קה

ליובאוויטש